SAVING CAN-DO

HOW TO REVIVE THE SPIRIT OF AMERICA

PHILIP K. HOWARD

RODIN BOOKS

Copyright © 2025 Philip K. Howard

All rights reserved.

No portion of this book may be reproduced in any fashion, print, facsimile, or electronic, or by any method yet to be developed, without the express written permission of the publisher.

"The Human Authority Needed for Good Schools," first published by Hoover Institution, Education Futures Council. Copyright Philip K. Howard © 2024

"Escape from Quicksand: A New Framework for Modernizing America," first published by Manhattan Institute. Copyright Philip K. Howard © 2025

Hardcover ISBN 978-1-957588-40-7
eBook ISBN 978-1-957588-41-4

PUBLISHED BY RODIN BOOKS INC.
666 Old Country Road
Suite 510
Garden City, New York 11530

www.rodinbooks.com

Book and cover design by Alexia Garaventa

Manufactured in the United States of America

Also by Philip K. Howard

The Death of Common Sense

The Collapse of the Common Good

Life Without Lawyers

The Rule of Nobody

Try Common Sense

Not Accountable

Everyday Freedom

SAVING CAN-DO

HOW TO REVIVE THE SPIRIT OF AMERICA

To the memory of

Gregory Davis Kennedy (1967–2025),

who epitomized the best of
American character—
smart, practical, fun, always helpful,
and always striving

CONTENTS

Introduction: Is This America's 1917 Moment?
1

Striving: How to Recover America's Magic
9

The Human Authority Needed for Good Schools
43

Escape from Quicksand: A New Framework
for Modernizing America
69

Notes
99

Acknowledgments
139

About the Author
141

INTRODUCTION
IS THIS AMERICA'S 1917 MOMENT?

All societies periodically undergo a major shift in the social order. These changes are often triggered by the failure of the ruling elite to deal with outside pressures, as in Russia in 1917.

America seems to be at one of those moments of change. Broad populist resentment has led to the takeover by Trump's MAGA movement of the Republican Party, and now Washington. The imperative for change is not limited to the MAGA half of the population. Almost two-thirds of Americans think Washington needs "very major reform."[1] Elon Musk's idea for a Department of Government Efficiency (DOGE) enjoyed broad popular support before losing steam amid big promises and small benefits.

Trump's approach is to swing a wrecking ball at the status quo—against wokeness, open borders, bloated bureaucracy, and paternalistic foreign policy. Trump has a kind of feral genius for sniffing out idiocies.

But where's Trump's vision of how government will work better the day after DOGE? Toppling the old order leaves a vacuum that, without a new vision, can be filled by unpredictable new ideas for governing, sometimes catastrophically, as with the Committee of Public Safety after the French Revolution or the Bolsheviks in Russia. Letting nature take its course after Trump's wrecking ball is unlikely to end well, leaving a wreckage of public agencies, perhaps replaced by an AI-driven autocracy that would exacerbate populist alienation.

Democrats are strangely quiet, apparently content to wait until Trump fails. This works fine for Democrats as a business model: Opposing Trump is all they need to raise buckets of money. Interest groups will pay a lot to defend the status quo, and Democrats have no agenda to cut red tape or public pork. But standing for the status quo against the tides of change is not likely to be a winning strategy, however much money is funneled into party coffers.

So here we are: Neither party has a vision for better government.[2] Democrats are in denial, waiting their turn to run a bloated government that Americans loathe. Trump and friends can sack Washington, but, as Rome learned long ago, the destruction of what's weak and corrupt can leave people worse off if there's no new plan. Retribution is a recipe for civil strife, not a governing strategy.

The governing vision that's needed, I think, should aim to deliver results, honor our humanity, and inspire leadership. Running a good school, building transmission lines, and clear-cutting healthcare bureaucracy aren't the hardest problems in human history. Letting Americans stride forward requires getting Big Brother off our backs, including for people with leadership responsibility. New choices and compromises to meet the challenges of our time will be far easier when the rest of the governing machinery works tolerably well.

The core of this new vision is a simpler framework of goals and principles, activated by humans using their judgment. Let people take responsibility again, and judge them by how they do. This is hardly radical—it's the operating framework of the Constitution. It's also how any good school or organization actually works. The proper role of law is to guard against transgressions of authority, not micromanage choices.

Nor is it partisan. Governing for results is aimed at practical implementation, not policy differences over, say, regulation vs. deregulation. Who doesn't want to fix poor schools, or cut red tape?

The order of change is to capture the public's imagination, not to somehow take control of a party. New visions can have a power of their own.[3] It doesn't take many legislators to dislodge the slim majorities in Congress. A few brave souls could break free and champion a new governing vision that, with popular demand, a majority of Congress could feel pressure to support.

The vision is this: Replace red tape with responsibility. Give leaders room to lead. Let us tackle local problems in our own ways. Let us interact honestly without the overhang of legal threats.

A simplified operating framework will empower officials to fix crumbling infrastructure, and extricate them from red tape for defense procurement and for healthcare. Administrative costs in healthcare, for example, now total over $10,000 per American family;[4] perhaps some of that could be redirected to more pressing public needs. A new human responsibility framework, within broad legal boundaries, will empower communities to figure things out for themselves.

Liberating Americans to take responsibility also promises a pot of gold, far more valuable than good government alone: It will reenergize America's can-do spirit. We can do things our own way. We can make a difference. Government built on the solid foundation of individual responsibility will inspire some people to become leaders. We can be rallied towards new goals and a better world. America's future greatness depends on empowering Americans to make our institutions work, not trading in Washington red tape for Washington autocracy.

Simpler governing frameworks activated by human responsibility would transform how government works at all levels of society. But replacing 1,000-page rulebooks and elaborate legal processes is not like pushing a button. New frameworks must accommodate public goals now micromanaged by thousands of laws and regulations.

Replacing the red tape state will be a decade-long project, akin to the reforms of the Progressive Era or in the 1960s. A massive legal and bureaucratic edifice has been erected over the past half century, dedicated to the proposition that all public choices should be strained through a legal sieve. Human judgment is in many settings illegal. People have been indoctrinated in the rote compliance model. Many public employees have no muscle memory of what it means to take responsibility. Accountability is a terrifying concept—isn't that a violation of individual rights?

Civil service must be completely overhauled to be a merit system, not a sinecure. Union controls over public management must be discarded, by constitutional challenges if necessary. How can democracy work if elected executives have no managerial authority? Oversight hierarchies must be created to build public trust. Officials need to be retrained. Pilot projects are needed to build public confidence.

Americans for years have enjoyed the luxury of outsourcing government to a permanent caste of insiders in Washington. We know the system is sluggish and unresponsive, but take comfort that it prevents big mistakes. A centralized bureaucracy is all we thought we needed. As Tocqueville observed:

> Centralization . . . maintains society in a *status quo* alike secure from improvement and decline; and perpetuates a drowsy regularity

in the conduct of affairs; . . . in short, it excels in prevention, but not in action. Its force deserts it when society is to be profoundly moved . . . [and] the secret of its impotence is disclosed.[5]

Americans have tolerated endemic public failures and inefficiencies for decades, probably because these failures coincided with a period of unparalleled national prosperity. Most of us could afford to look the other way. We could avoid the conflict and hard choices that go along with changing governing structures. Then we got MAGA.

Now the world order is in perilous disarray, and Trump is smashing the drowsy bureaucracies with nothing to replace them.

Change is difficult. That's why it rarely happens without a crisis. But crisis is not the time to rethink basic understandings. Americans have been indoctrinated with flawed ideas on how to govern.[6] We must discard the sacred cows of current legal orthodoxy—including the preoccupation with rote compliance, objective proof, and a lowest common denominator concept of individual rights.

The three essays in this book describe the fatal flaws in our understanding of how to govern and present a new governing vision:

1. "Striving" looks back to the core elements of America's can-do culture. It then deconstructs

the assumptions propping up the current system and explains why, for example, bureaucratic detail causes people to fail, and why subjective judgments are the essence of freedom, not its enemy.

2. In "The Human Authority Needed for Good Schools," originally published by the Hoover Institution, I explain how school reform efforts have ignored the core trait of all good schools—a school culture grounded in individual responsibility. Most reform efforts have unwittingly undermined healthy school cultures with top-down controls. It is almost impossible to transform K–12 education until teachers, principals, and the communities they serve are liberated from red tape and union controls.

3. "Escape from Quicksand," originally published by the Manhattan Institute, explains how conventions of legal compliance have caused infrastructure permitting reforms to fail. It provides a blueprint for new governing frameworks that would enable officials to approve projects, to procure commercially reasonable contracts, and, belatedly, to start rebuilding America's crumbling infrastructure.

No one knows when the stars will align for big change. But the ground is shaking, and a coherent new governing vision will be indispensable when the time comes. The red tape state has failed. I describe here why its underlying assumptions were flawed, and propose a new framework built on the solid foundation of individual responsibility.

STRIVING
HOW TO RECOVER AMERICA'S MAGIC

Americans are strivers. That's the main power of our culture. We can be whatever we want to be, as long as we can pull it off. Waking up in the morning, Americans can strive to achieve our goals in our own ways. Freedom in America is not just free speech, voting suffrage, and protections against state coercion. Freedom in America is the power to invent yourself, and to take ownership for your actions and relations with society.

America's culture of striving was born of exiles and explorers confronting the challenges of the wilderness. Americans were not locked in to predetermined paths of the old world. We formed our own communities, with our own values. Unlocking human potential proved powerful not only for the colonists but also for later arrivals. Immigrants two centuries after the Puritans not only worked their way to a better life, but sometimes achieved greatness and riches, where their ancestors had been peasant farmers for a thousand years. Leaving aside the shameful exceptions, American culture empowered individuals "to make the best of themselves."[1] None of this came easily, and the field of freedom is covered with broken dreams. But freedom in America means participating in a giant marketplace of human potential. The dynamic of success is to convince other free people to want your product, your skills, and your character. People succeed, economist Friedrich Hayek observed, "according to what others think."[2]

The human energy unleashed by all these self-directed Americans, Tocqueville observed, was our defining trait: "Men are never stationary; a thousand chances waft them to and fro." Governing in America similarly meant "all-pervading and restless activity," which may not result in "the most skillful government" but can also "produce wonders."[3]

This spirit of America has been collapsing over the past fifty years. Americans no longer feel free to follow their instincts, or even to be themselves in daily dealings. That's because of a flawed philosophy of governing—that law should preempt human judgment in daily choices.[4]

This legal philosophy was an effort, after the tumultuous 1960s, to avoid any more abuses of human authority such as racism and pollution. There was "a massive redefinition of freedom" after the 1960s, historian Eric Foner found, "as a rejection of all authority."[5] The target of reform was human fallibility. No abuses would be possible if officials could no longer exercise their judgment. The authority of officials, employers, teachers, and others with responsibility was replaced with a kind of legal software program designed to regularize and purify daily choices—prescriptive rules, extensive processes, and rights to challenge their decisions.

For over fifty years, this legal experiment has tried to create a governing and legal system better than people. New rules are continually written to cover new situations, new rights invented to challenge the exercise of human judgment, and legal disclosures such as environmental reviews have burgeoned to thousands of pages. Avoiding value judgments, criticisms, or other manifestations of personal belief became a social norm in the workplace. What matters is what you can prove by objective facts.

Instead of doing what they think best, Americans have been trained to focus on compliance and avoiding legal risks. Instead of striding forward with energy and excitement, Americans get stuck in a kind of legal quicksand. Instead of making government better and society fairer, this unrelenting attention to law has resulted in public failure and social resentment:

- Public officials feel powerless to cut through paralytic red tape, or to manage public departments sensibly. Projects to modernize infrastructure, for example, can take a decade or longer.

- Candor in the workplace is virtually extinct, supplanted by a culture of fear that an offhand comment might be held against you.
- Universities are a hornet's nest of legal demands and accusations, bloated with compliance personnel, and no longer confident to uphold values of excellence.
- Failing schools can't be fixed because of red tape and union controls. Instead of maintaining order in the classroom, teachers worry about proving fairness in a legal hearing.
- Instead of letting the children go out and play by themselves, parents worry about lawsuits if something goes wrong.
- Leadership at all levels has been hollowed into a compliance job, allowing room for judgment only after navigating the legal labyrinth. Instead of feeling free to make judgments about moral character, for example, managers and officials are told to avoid being "judgmental" and to stick to platitudes.[6]

Nothing much works as it should. Like pouring acid over our culture, law everywhere has corroded the spirit of America. Tocqueville warned us:

> It is especially dangerous to enslave men in the minor details of life. For my own part, I should be inclined to think freedom less

necessary in great things than in little ones . . . Subjection in minor affairs . . . does not drive men to resistance, but it crosses them at every turn, till they are led to surrender the exercise of their own will. Thus their spirit is gradually broken and their character enervated.[7]

Many Americans have now had enough, and want to burst free. Public ineptitude and a broad sense of repression open the door for authoritarian leaders who promise to make the trains run on time, whatever it takes.

The better option is to revive America's can-do culture. But this requires an intervention to abandon the post-1960s experiment in legal micromanagement. Law must be pulled back into its traditional role of safeguarding against violations of law, not dictating daily choices and mediating human relations.

The Elements of a Striving Culture

The core element of America's culture is self-ownership. We own who we are—our goals, our skills, our values, and how we do things and relate to others. Individual ownership of our choices energizes our instincts and imagination.

This ownership of ourselves is also the basis for self-esteem—not only doing things our own way, but also displaying our character—to do what's right and fair, and to act in ways that earn the respect of others. The "pursuit of happiness" in the Declaration of Independence came from Scottish enlightenment theologian Francis Hutcheson, who argued that personal fulfilment was derived in large part by how we help others.[8]

Individual ownership translates into community ownership. We're better together, joining with others for barn-raisings, civic activities, and social services. Tocqueville saw this sense of community ownership as acting in our "self-interest, rightly understood."[9]

A paradox of American individuality is that it is the foundation for mutual trust. Good character is an asset—not just virtue for its own sake, but the key that opens the door to many opportunities. People succeed, generally, because other people value their work and trust them.

Not everyone succeeds, of course, or displays good character. But America kept surging forward, even as its cultural traditions became more diverse, because the shared value of responsibility tends to leave untrustworthy people behind, no longer accepted by the people they dealt with. American freedom provides a marketplace for good character as well as individual achievement—"a most conspicuous Theatre," as George Washington predicted in 1783, "which seems to be peculiarly designated by Providence for the display of human greatness and felicity."[10]

The legal concepts destroying America's spirit are based on flawed assumptions about human success and social cohesion. I discuss each of these in turn: how bureaucracy interferes with accomplishment, why the quest for objective validation disables human judgment, how forced politeness destroys mutual trust, why authority should replace red tape, and why people judging people is the foundation for a moral society.

The Freedom Needed for Accomplishment

The first virtue of America's striving culture is accomplishment. Americans roll up their sleeves and get things done. No other culture produced anything like it. Inventors who changed the world came from nowhere. Thomas Edison, with almost no formal education, tinkered and intuited his way to harnessing electricity, creating a light bulb, and recording sound. At a time when the leading physicists in the world were competing to achieve manned flight, two bicycle mechanics in Dayton, Ohio, were rigging airfoils on bicycle handlebars to test the properties of lift.[11] Steve Jobs was a college dropout who had an interest in calligraphy.

Getting things done is generally intuitive, not logical. Most people don't think their way to success. They go through "the usual process of unconscious trial and error by which we *feel our way* to success," philosopher scientist Michael Polanyi explains, "without specifiably knowing how we do it." Studies of a wide range of activities—of chess grandmasters, carpenters, waiters—confirm that their decisions come from their subconscious, not conscious decisions. Getting things done, Professor Mike Rose found, is an immersive activity: People "disappear . . . into the task." For most decisions, our knowledge is in our action.[12]

Enter law. Until the 1960s, law's role was providing a kind of legal fence to safeguard against misconduct. The outside of the legal fence protected against antisocial conduct, such as crime. The inside of the legal fence defined an open field of freedom where people are free to do as they wish. Philosopher Isaiah Berlin characterized this legal fence as "frontiers, not artificially drawn, within which men should be inviolable."[13]

The area of "inviolable" freedom no longer exists. Law's single-minded focus since the 1960s has been to prescribe in advance rules and procedures for anything that might go wrong—an "almost lawless passion for lawmaking," in the words of historian Henry Steele Commager.[14] Instead of a framework for freedom, law became a massive monument to the precautionary principle. For half a century, new laws and regulations have piled on top of old laws to try to codify solutions to potential problems and mistakes.

The theory of injecting law into daily choices was to guarantee fairness and avoid mistakes, and thereby enhance freedom. But the effect is to yank people out of their intuitive ability to get things done.

Detailed legal rules can rarely be internalized, and require conscious effort to keep straight. The problem is that the "working memory" of humans—the conscious part of the brain—can process only a few new things at once. In computer terms, working memory is tiny, like an 8-bit processor: "minute in its ability to process new material." But it has prodigious capacity to "process very extensive and complex, previously learned information" that is contained in long-term memory, the subconscious part of the brain. Our skills are internalized in long-term memory and constitute what we think of as "understanding." Without any conscious volition on our part, the "hidden nature of long-term memory" is drawn into working memory as needed.[15]

Research by psychologist John Sweller and others shows that the conscious effort required to address detailed bureaucracy often exhausts the capacity of working memory. The resulting "cognitive overload" limits the human ability to draw on the intelligence of long-term memory. Bureaucracy, in other words, tends to make people go brain dead.[16]

The caricature of the soulless bureaucrat, recounted in countless novels and studies, is grounded in the limitations of human cognition to deal with dictates that cannot be internalized into long-term memory. Bureaucrats plodding through compliance checklists lose connection to empathy and problem-solving.*

Research across a broad range of human endeavor demonstrates how bureaucracy undermines the capacity of people to do their jobs. Professor Richard Arum, in his study of the effects of law on school disorder, found that worry about due process requirements had the effect of disorienting teachers from maintaining control: "It is this hesitation, doubt, and weakening of conviction . . . that has undermined the effectiveness of school discipline."[17]

Freedom is supposed to provide an open zone of inviolable choices, not a legal checklist. Striving requires people to be free to "disappear into their task," not continually look into a legal mirror to

---

* The heartless bureaucrat is famously depicted in fiction by Dickens, Balzac, Kafka, Gogol, and Heller, to name just a few. Some observers see it as personality flaw, and others as a necessary element of doing the job—for example, Max Weber: "Bureaucracy develops the more perfectly, the more it is 'dehumanized.'" But studies of cognitive overload suggest that bureaucrats preoccupied with rules actually lack the capacity to respond to the situation before them. Cognitive overload not only impedes drawing on what Nobel laureate Daniel Kahneman called "system 2" thinking—that is, questioning assumptions and reflecting on long-term implications—but also impedes access to what Kahneman called "system 1" thinking—that is, drawing on their instincts and heuristics to make intuitive judgments.

Professor William Simon tells the story of the bureaucratic clerk who refused to restore welfare to a desperate mother who filed the application late. The clerk asserted to the mother: "There is nothing I can do." In fact, the error could have readily been fixed by an official in an adjoining office. What the clerk was thinking was that there was nothing that she could personally do. But in the mental cubicle of bureaucratic rules, all the clerk thought about was her own compliance, not solving the dire predicament of the young mother before her. This might be called "system zero" thinking, where mental capacity focuses on artificial constraints instead of instincts, norms, or public goals.[a]

check on compliance. In the zone of freedom, people should be free to pursue their dreams, live their values, draw on their instincts, and interact freely with others. People in the free zone should be accountable not to law but to the decisions by other free people.

The test of effective law, John Locke suggested, is not how much it controls, but whether it enhances the overall scope of our freedom.[18] The obsessive drive to foreclose anything that might go wrong has left little room for the freedom to make things go right. Instead of perfecting freedom, law replaced freedom—guaranteeing frustration and failure.

Subjectivity Is the Essence of Freedom, Not the Enemy

The post-1960s complex of rules, processes, and rights has been designed with one overriding operational premise—to preempt human judgment. The defect in human judgment, the theory goes, is that it is tainted with subjectivity. People should not be allowed to assert their beliefs, especially if they affect someone else. Here is the motto for our time: Who am I to judge?[19]

But subjectivity is the main feature of freedom, not a bug that justifies a legal takeover of human judgment. Our subjective beliefs are in large part who we are, as individuals, as participants in an institution, and as a society. Subjectivity is not random but is the manifestation of the American spirit.

Good judgment is not objective. There's an irreducible subjective quality to our choices. Our judgment is formed by perceptions, experience, training, values, and biases that cannot be sorted into component parts. Human judgment is fallible, of course, which is why organizations often run important decisions by others.

Avoiding human judgment, on the other hand, is like wearing a blindfold. Life situations are too varied to be prescribed in advance by objective criteria. Because "the world, like a kaleidoscope, never exactly repeats any previous situation," Michael Polanyi explained, "we can achieve consistency only by identifying manifestly different situations . . . and this requires a series of personal judgments."[20]

Governing sensibly is impossible if officials can't use their judgment—regulatory choices almost always involve trade-off judgments that cannot be codified in advance. Do the benefits of a transmission line outweigh the harm of building through a pristine forest? That's a value judgment, not a decision enhanced by years of legal argument.

Judgments about people require human perception, not just objective and provable criteria. How do you prove that someone doesn't try hard, or cooperate, or is selfish? How does a school principal prove that a teacher is boring and ineffective?

Nor can academic and cultural excellence be dissected into objective parts. "Good expert judgment is generally of an intuitive nature," psychologist

Gerd Gigerenzer notes, and cannot be demonstrated by "after-the-fact justifications." Other than in hard sciences, academics can't prove by objective evidence what's good, thoughtful, and well written. Nor can they prove that they're not biased. But lack of objective proof doesn't make their expert judgments invalid. "What we reject about the words *objective* and *subjective*," Philip Jackson and colleagues observed in their study of teachers, *The Moral Life of Schools*, "is the implication that one refers to something real and the other does not."[21]

Deciding only by objective criteria generally guarantees unfairness—"exalting what we can know and prove," philosopher Michael Polanyi observed, "while covering up . . . all that we know and cannot prove." Like water finding a crack, people quickly learn to frame their self-interest in legalistic terms:

- Government procurement procedures favor inferior vendors who know how to "game" the so-called objective criteria.
- Public permitting can be dragged out indefinitely by parties known to have an ulterior motive, for example, to get financial benefits by agreeing to drop their objections.
- Due process hearings for teacher termination have little to do with their performance, and become exercises in legal sophistry—in one case, whether the school could prove by objective evidence

whether the teacher had been told to grade student work.

- Broad resentment at DEI programs is not generally based on giving everyone a fair shot, but how DEI worked—compelling a supervisor to prove a negative. How can a supervisor prove that the DEI candidate is not as good as another candidate?[22]

Instead of a brave new world of pure objectivity, what's replaced subjectivity are the subjective values of whoever's not in charge. Who's to say that a Rembrandt is more compelling than a contemporary painting? Finger-pointing about bad values in prior eras is used to discredit cultural achievements from the same period. No pillar of our culture is safe from the assault on subjectivity. Why do Caucasians and Asians score better on standardized tests? Who wrote those tests? Attacking values on the basis that they're merely values, without any generally accepted values to replace them, is wanton destruction.[23]

A counter-assault on DEI is now pushing institutions towards the opposite values. First we had the DEI Stasi: where my freedom belongs not to me but to the sensitivities of whomever I deal with. Do you feel unsafe? Maybe just scrap *King Lear* and *Huckleberry Finn*. Now we're telling universities what to teach and law firms whom they can represent, and deporting foreign students who demonstrate for the wrong cause. Freedom is forgotten as the culture plummets towards opposing visions of the lowest common denominator.

"Subjectivity," Pope John Paul II observed, is "a kind of synonym for the irreducible in the human being."[24] Subjectivity is what freedom is supposed to empower. Society too depends on empowerment of subjective norms that most citizens accept. Without subjectivity, the levers of social order become empty gestures. Job evaluations and recommendations say little or nothing. Grade inflation makes grades meaningless. Wisdom of the ages is supplanted by an obligation to endure new art, music, literature, and history on the basis, mainly, that it was made by someone else.

Subjectivity is not license to let the imagination run wild. Facts still matter. Reasonableness is a standard by which people will be held accountable. But human judgment and cultural values are unavoidably subjective. Subjectivity is who we are.

Let Us Be: Purge Law from Human Relations

Healthy relationships, energetic institutions, and America's can-do culture all ultimately hinge on our freedom in personal interactions.

Trusting relationships are earned through action and honest dealings. Trust is almost impossible without spontaneity, which Hannah Arendt considered the "most elementary manifestation of human freedom." People readily perceive lack of honesty in the stilted language of political correctness. Building trust is impossible, philosopher Onora O'Neill observes, when people don't feel free to be honest or true to themselves.[25]

Law has poisoned human relations in most institutional settings. That's because it's easy to challenge someone's judgment or motives, and almost impossible to disprove those accusations. Americans will do almost anything to avoid being accused of racism or other bias. Yet we also know that humans are wired to rationalize any disappointing decision as unfair.

The predictable result is to chill daily relations. Mandatory training in the workplace has one overriding message: Don't be yourself. Watch your words. Avoid spontaneity at all costs. The goal is to avoid giving offense. Instead we corroded the basis for human trust and understanding, and exacerbated the bias it is intended to avoid.[26]

By subjecting personnel decisions to legal scrutiny, law corroded the basis for mutual trust, and nurtured a new norm of what might be called non-honesty. In black-white relations, sociologist Orlando Patterson observed, no one "dares say what he or she really means."[27] The loss of candor fuels the growth of suspicion. Why did someone get promoted instead of another? How about the bonuses?

We know how we got here: America's history of racism makes us eager to lean over backwards to avoid discrimination. Law has proved reasonably effective to break down historical patterns of discrimination. But law can't decide who's good and who's not. People are all different. Institutional needs are different. Injecting law into individual personnel decisions is the recipe for distrust, not the cure.

Deciding who's good at what is astonishingly complex. As psychologists Barry Schwartz and Kenneth Sharpe describe in their book *Practical Wisdom*, achievement often hinges on "character traits like loyalty, self-control, . . . perseverance, integrity, open-mindedness, thoroughness, and kindness."[28]

Yet co-workers generally know who's good and who's not. Mutual trust in a workplace requires a general sense that these decisions are made fairly, including that people are held to the same standards. In *The Moral Life of Schools*, a study of the intangible factors that distinguish effective teachers, professor Philip Jackson and colleagues found that "laying aside all exceptions . . . there is typically a lot of truth in the judgments we make of others."[29]

Trust can never be restored until people feel free to interact honestly. Of course people will disagree. It's a free country. Of course some people will be unfair, or rude, perhaps even offensive. But most of those people will pay the price for their conduct. The benefits of accepting occasional poor behavior far outweigh the harms: Restoring honesty in human relations will enhance understanding, trust, and success across society.

Letting people interact freely should not be considered a novel risk for a society organized on the principle of individual freedom. Any healthy organization strives to avoid unfairness. Honest feedback causes pain, but failure is also the main way people learn.[30] Letting people be spontaneous means some will put their feet in their mouths, but their authenticity is also a basis for trust. Let them apologize. Yes, all humans have implicit biases. But, for most people, biases diminish when we get to know each other. Good workers and helpful colleagues tend to do well, whatever their identity group or background.

But what about individual rights? People assert individual rights as protection against insidious motives. But, as noted earlier, there's no legal CT scan that can sort out the countless strands that form human judgment, so the possibility of a claim has rendered honesty extinct in workplace interactions. This idea of individual rights against employers also turns upside down the constitutional concept of rights. Instead of protecting against the coercive power of the state, these new rights invoke the state's coercive power—that's what a lawsuit is—to repudiate the freedom of supervisors to use their judgment.†

Fairness in decisions about particular people is beyond the capacity of law. Fairness to one person is unfairness in the eyes of another. Making these judgments is an unavoidable aspect of collective activity. Scrutinizing personal judgments through a lens of objective proof, on the other hand, fosters a mindset of grievance and entitlement. The person left behind assumes the choice was either discrimination or reverse discrimination.

For decades now, law has aimed to guarantee equality—anything to make up for past sins. But there's no happy place over the hill. Believing that equality is a matter of objective proof or entitlement is a sure formula for disappointment and bitterness.[31] Instead of bringing people together, the legal quest for fairness in individual decisions has created a society riven with distrust.

---

† Civil service and public schools have become accountability-free zones, where practically any supervisory decision can be challenged as a violation of the employee's rights. Public unions argue that putting supervisors to the proof of the fairness of their personnel decisions is just a matter of Due Process. But the effect is to invert the hierarchy of authority; the burden is now on the public supervisor to prove the correctness of his supervisory decisions. Instead of being held to a standard of serving the public, public servants now demand, in essence, that the public should serve them. As a result, government in key respects is unmanageable. It is now basically impossible, for example, to terminate a public employee for incompetence. It is also difficult to instill energy and pride into public culture when everyone knows that job performance doesn't matter. Democracy can't function if officials lack the managerial authority to fulfill their constitutional responsibilities. I discuss these issues in my book *Not Accountable*.

The only cure is to remove legal fear so people can interact honestly. Except for tortious conduct, such as sexual harassment or other misconduct, law should be pulled away from human relations. Law can still protect against patterns or practices of discrimination, but "in our face-to-face interactions," Professor Orlando Patterson concluded, we "should treat each other exactly alike" and not with "any special set of sensitivities."[32]

Striving Requires Authority for Leaders

America needs leadership. That's what everyone says. But leadership is just an empty word if people in charge lack the authority to act on their judgment.

The disempowerment of authority in the name of individual rights has led, ironically, to the loss of freedom by individuals. Most human activities are in institutions—at the workplace, in communities, and in government. Our striving depends upon leaders setting direction and upholding the integrity of institutional standards and values. Without leadership, group activities become scrums of people milling around.

Leadership of a department or institution is not everything, but almost. Leadership is necessary to allocate resources, to innovate, and to keep people rowing together. Well-managed organizations are materially more productive than poorly managed ones.[33]

Collaboration is enhanced by the camaraderie of people with a shared loyalty to a common goal. Because institutions are populated with people who don't know each other well, shared trust requires a general belief that leaders of the organizations will uphold common standards and values. In any organization, management theorist Peter Drucker observed, there have to be "people who make decisions . . . who are accountable for the organization's mission, its spirit, its performance, its results."[34]

In the age of individual rights, no one talks about the rights of institutions or institutional leaders. But nothing can work effectively, including democracy and individual freedom itself, unless people in charge have authority to fulfill their responsibilities.

Authority in government. Government has coercive power, so the Framers took care to delineate its authority and provide safeguards against abuse. But they also understood that government can't do its job sensibly without the continual exercise of judgment by officials, public employees, and judges.[35]

Governing fairly and effectively requires officials who can strive to meet common goals. Good schools require principals to have authority to uphold standards and teachers to feel ownership of the classroom. Modernizing infrastructure requires officials to have authority to make timely judgments on what and how to build. Regulatory oversight requires judgments on priorities and practicalities, not mindless compliance.

The authority in government that's most important to a functioning society is distributed authority to officials at all levels of responsibility, not authoritarian dictates from the top.[36]

Judges too must don the cloak of freedom's guardians—not to second-guess governing choices that are politically accountable, but to make sure officials do not transgress the boundaries of their authority. Judges must also make legal rulings to keep lawsuits within reasonable boundaries, so that legal exposure, to quote Oliver Wendell Holmes, Jr., "correspond[s] to the actual feelings and demands of the community."[37] Otherwise fear of lawsuits undermines freedoms throughout society.[‡]

[‡] The current practice in America, particularly in accident cases, is that people can sue for almost anything. Instead of enhancing freedom, this open season approach to lawsuits causes freedom to be replaced by defensiveness. That's why the landscape of our free society is littered with warnings for everything ("Caution, Contents Are Hot"), why hospitals squander billions in "defensive medicine," and why employers in the land of the First Amendment no longer give job references.

Law's consistency is a foundational requirement of a free society—"similar cases should be decided alike." Otherwise no one knows where they stand. Consistency requires restoring the authority of judges to make legal rulings on the boundaries of claims, not leaving verdicts on social standards to, as Oliver Wendell Holmes, Jr., put it, the "whim of the particular jury." Juries are generally sensible, but they have no authority to set legal precedent. "An act is illegal," Professor Donald Black observed, "if it is *vulnerable* to legal action."

Nor, as commonly asserted, does the Seventh Amendment preclude judicial rulings that draw legal boundaries on which claims can go to a jury. The Seventh Amendment explicitly acknowledges that civil claims are subject to "the rules of the common law." Holmes admonished judges to make rulings: "Negligence . . . [is] a standard of conduct, a standard which we hold the parties bound to know beforehand."[b]

Because governing choices involve state power, checks and balances are prudent to inspire public trust and avoid abuse. These checks also require exercise of human judgment, whether by superior officials, courts, or legislatures.

By contrast, the premise of post-1960s governing philosophy is that freedom is enhanced by removing official judgment altogether—the less authority by officials, the more freedom for us. The wreckage of this failed philosophy lies all around us. The rules and procedures designed to proscribe authority have supplanted individual freedom and saddled America with a trifecta of failed government: legal micromanagement that makes government "authentically incompetent," red tape that chokes citizen and business initiative, and a dreary public culture that repels good people from public service. Who wants to spend their life pushing paper?[38]

Federal law and regulation now totals about 150 million words, nearly all imposed since the 1960s in the quest to control every decision of public interest. Instead of using common sense, officials enforce rigid rules that matter to no one—like not having a "material safety data sheet" for Joy dishwashing liquid, or doing a study of historic buildings for an infrastructure project affecting no buildings.[39]

Governing without judgment suffocates society. Because of reimbursement and regulatory micromanagement, doctors and nurses spend almost half their day doing deskwork. Special ed teachers are similarly swamped. Endemic social problems such as homelessness remain endemic because no official has authority to override the rigid legal silos.[40]

Bureaucracy breeds more bureaucracy: Universities, employers, and government itself are bloated with administrators whose main job is to fill out forms and others to check to make sure the forms were filled out.[41] All this red tape, disconnected from human intuition, is exhausting and contributes to the epidemic of burnout.

Progressive thought leaders have awoken to the harm of public paralysis, and are calling for doing what it takes to achieve "abundance." They don't have a vision for reform, however, and their rhetoric suggests that the solution lies in cutting back some of the red tape. Pruning the red tape jungle can never work, however. No matter how much is pruned, whatever legal rules are left will still preempt human judgment. Reforms to catch fraud and waste haven't worked because privacy laws prevent agencies from sharing data. Reforms purporting to limit the time for infrastructure permitting haven't worked—because the time limits get stalled by multiple mandates to allow participation by Native American tribes, protect historic buildings, and so forth.[42]

The red tape jungle must be abandoned, not pruned. The flaw is in the premise—that law should preempt the judgment of officials. The proper role of law is to delineate authority, including oversight and accountability, not to shackle officials with bureaucratic central planning. What's required is a shift in operating philosophy, from rote compliance back to the human responsibility model contemplated by the Framers. As James Madison put it:

> It is one of the most prominent features of the constitution, a principle that pervades the whole system, that there should be the highest possible degree of responsibility in all the Executive officers thereof.[43]

A more practical framework consists mainly of goals and principles, like the Constitution, all of 7,500 words. For example, upwards of a thousand worker safety rules could be replaced by this general principle: "Tools and equipment shall be reasonably suited for the use intended, in accord with industry standards." Homebuilders would know to use industrial-grade hammers, but the bookkeeper could use a lightweight hammer for hanging pictures.

The optimum amount of legal precision depends on the context. Social Security eligibility should be precise. But in most matters involving human relations and regulatory approvals, governing by principles has the virtue of allowing people to use common sense in the immediate circumstances. Nor does leaving room for judgment give officials carte blanche or unfettered discretion. The simpler framework of principles would set the boundaries of official authority, and provide mechanisms for accountability and oversight, just as the Constitution does.

Reempowering official judgment will unleash human initiative within government and throughout society. Government and schools can be manageable again. The defense department will be more agile. Infrastructure can be modernized. Social problems such as homelessness can be addressed. Children will be allowed to go out and play without fear of legal consequences. Citizens will be energized because local communities will be empowered to solve problems in a local way.

This legal transformation will be resisted by interest groups feeding at the bureaucratic trough, and therefore feasible only with overwhelming public demand. Nor can it be designed with a few backroom deals. Successful efforts to clean out the legal stables almost always happen the same way: a small committee of experts is charged with making a proposal. Area by area, Congress should appoint "recodification commissions" to propose simpler frameworks that revive human authority and accountability.[44]

To get infrastructure and housing going in the meantime, Congress can enact temporary frameworks that bypass the current legal thicket: "Notwithstanding any law to the contrary, permits for new transmission lines shall be awarded on the following basis. . . ."[45]

Reclaiming Morality in American Culture

Doing what's right, or responsible, has little connection to legality. The role of law is mainly defensive—to protect against social harms. Morality, on the other hand, is the practice of doing good. While law sets the framework for a free society, moral character within that framework is the basis for trust, and therefore usually a prerequisite for sustained success.

It would be hard to find any successful society, or institution, that doesn't have a culture of shared values and mutual trust. Societies with shared values reap the benefits of high "social capital"—greater cooperation and social bonds, innovation, and general happiness. A former British high court judge, Lord Moulton, argued that an "obedience to . . . unenforceable" values is the essential hallmark of a healthy culture: "the whole realm which recognizes the sway of duty, fairness, sympathy, taste, and all the other things that make life beautiful and society possible."[46]

The moral fabric of American society has been fraying for several decades. Political scientist Alan Wolfe found that Americans had "lost the distinction between right and wrong and desperately want it back." Diagnoses vary, but legal micromanagement is a root cause. In his 1978 Harvard commencement speech Aleksandr Solzhenitsyn observed that life without law was bad, as in the Soviet Union, but that a society of too much law lost its morality:

> But a society with no other scale but the legal one is also less than worthy of man. A society based on the letter of the law and never reaching any higher fails to take advantage of the full range of human possibilities. The letter of the law is too cold and formal to have a beneficial influence on society. Whenever the tissue of life is woven of legalistic relationships, this creates an atmosphere of spiritual mediocrity that paralyzes man's noblest impulses.[47]

Czech playwright Václav Havel, another observer of apathy under the Soviets, warned against "the dreary standardization and rationalism" of legal regimentation.[48]

The more law prescribes daily choices, the less room there is for people to ask: "What's the right thing to do here?" Thick rulebooks breed a culture of compliance, in which people no longer even ask what's right. Whatever is lawful, they come to assume, is also morally permissible.

How can we reactivate morality in a culture smothered by legal dictates? Simplifying law to leave room for human judgment is a necessary step. Another change, which can start immediately, is for people to start debating policy and decision in moral terms.

The most powerful lever for morality is to judge people by their character. These judgments are not about purity but about how people relate to each other and the world. Morality is a way of living, not a litmus test. "The force of character," Emerson observed, "is cumulative." People in their actions reveal who they are. "My lived experience discloses not only my actions," as Pope John Paul II put it, "but also my inner happenings."[49]

People judging people is the main mechanism for a moral culture. Otherwise, morality is just smoke. Does this person act in a way we respect and trust? Or is he self-serving? People who are selfish or antisocial should lose our votes, or lose their jobs, or lose our friendship. Robert Reich argues, correctly, that people must fear being "shamed."[50] America's can-do culture was built on the broad trust on the validity of these judgments.

The moral decline in America has not been uniform, and social capital remains high in communities bound together by customs and traditions. These communities demonstrate the power of shared values. Mormons go to Utah, Hasidic Jews to Brooklyn, Scandinavians to Minnesota, techies to Silicon Valley, and so forth. What's valued in one community, or one university, need not be valued in another.[51]

The freedom to live our values, and to associate with those who share our values, is the main strength of our pluralistic society. The dynamic of striving naturally culminates in a diversity of communities. Each of these communities has its own moral integrity. The resulting trust of shared values within these groups is like rocket fuel for human initiative.

Introducing diverse perspectives can also be healthy, keeping everyone on their toes. Diversity in itself is not the goal, however, and, political scientist Robert Putnam found, tends to produce lower levels of trust.[52]

What kills morality is the subjugation of subjectivity—that personal values should be disregarded in public choices. The quest for an objective governing system, Havel observed, guaranteed its failure: "We are looking for an objective way out of the crisis of objectivism."[53]

The only cure, Havel concluded, is for people to embrace and demand individual agency at all levels of society: "Human uniqueness, human action, and the human spirit must be rehabilitated . . . Salvation can come only through a profound awakening of man to his own personal responsibility."[54]

Striving Requires Personal Authority

For almost four centuries, America has built a culture in which individuals can strive to develop and fulfill all that is within them—unleashing what Hayek called the "boundless variety of human nature—the wide range of individual capacities and potentialities."[55]

The magic of individual initiative is realized only in a dynamic marketplace. American freedom is not about compliance, objective proof, and, even less, entitlement. American freedom is the opportunity to participate in a marketplace—not only for business, but for democracy, for values of all sorts, and for morality. Our success or disappointments will be determined in this free marketplace.[56]

To be clear, the marketplace of a free society requires a reliable legal and governing framework. Social support can also reduce fear and enhance freedom. But extruding daily choices through the eye of a legal needle squeezes the life out of freedom. The aspiration to prescribe all that's good, and proscribe all that's bad, shuts down human initiative and values. This failure is not just a matter of degree, but of concept: Law has replaced freedom to act on your judgment.

America needs to replace the post-1960s governing philosophy, and its dreary aspiration for uniform compliance. But what is the new philosophy? A society cannot prosper unless "the minds of all the citizens ... [are] held together by certain predominant ideas."[57] Leaders must have authority to uphold the values of this new philosophy, or else it will just be words blowing in the wind.

The shift required is both traditional and radical: Replace red tape with individual responsibility. Empower leaders to make choices needed for society to move forward. Empower citizens to use their judgment to strive towards their goals. Empower everyone to judge the performance and character of everyone else. That's how a free society is supposed to work.

Red tape is strangling the goose of American striving. The new governing framework must be an open framework, activated by human judgment on the spot. Law should set goals and principles, and provide a structure of authority and accountability. Actual decisions within this framework are made by Americans taking responsibility. The aspiration is not mainly to deregulate—although American regulation is long overdue for a spring cleaning. The critical change is to a governing system that empowers officials and citizens alike to use their judgment.

Pulling the plug on the red tape state will transform America. A torrent of human initiative will be released throughout society when Americans no longer tiptoe through the day looking over their shoulders. Government can finally begin to meet its goals when officials can use their judgment.

New governing frameworks should be remade generally in accord with the following principles:

- Protecting individual freedom is the first goal of law. Law should affirmatively define and defend the scope of reasonable freedoms—not micromanage how to do things or lean over backwards to accommodate the disappointments or ideologies of claimants.

- Regulations should be knowable by the people expected to abide by them. In many areas, this will require simpler codes of guiding principles that are written to conform to common sense notions of right and wrong.

- Regulations should leave room for officials to make judgments about trade-offs and other considerations—for example, on scope of environmental review and timeliness of decisions. Instead of rote compliance, most regulatory frameworks should define the scope of official authority, and provide oversight by other officials. Governing sensibly requires officials to take responsibility for results, not just go by the book.

- Except for tortious behavior, such as fraud or sexual misconduct, law should not intercede in personal relations. Private antidiscrimination claims should be limited to patterns and practices of discrimination, not choices about one person.

- Fear is the enemy of freedom. One of the main goals of law is to reduce fear. Instead, by overprotecting against possible wrongs, law is now a source of fear—a Sword of Damocles hanging over social activities. Impartial judicial forums are necessary but not sufficient protections for Americans to feel free in daily dealings. To support freedom, law must be predictable, which requires courts and regulators to use their judgment to keep legal boundaries aligned with social norms.[58]

Remaking America's governing framework is an ambition of historic proportions, but it's hard to see any alternative. Our utopian legal experiment hasn't worked, resulting in public paralysis, a culture of selfishness and antipathy, and a reflexive grasp for authoritarian alternatives. Leaders in our constitutional order are largely powerless. Practical solutions are illegal. Legal argument has replaced the plain language of right and wrong.

The downward spiral of divisive politics and democratic cynicism will worsen as long as public failure persists and frustrated Americans feel powerless. The only cure is to restore to Americans their personal, institutional, and moral agency. Let Americans roll up their sleeves and act like Americans again.

THE HUMAN AUTHORITY NEEDED FOR GOOD SCHOOLS

Good schools require, more than anything, genuine human engagement. Each student has a different aptitude and needs. Each teacher must have the autonomy to connect with students and to earn moral authority. Each principal must assert and enforce common values and standards that everyone knows and can trust.

A school's culture is the sum of these countless human judgments and interactions. An effective school will generally have a culture where students feel cared for and inspired to do their best, where teachers feel a sense of ownership for their classrooms, and where principals have fostered a common feeling of aspiration and mutual trust.

I argue here that the endemic failure of America's public schools is due, more than anything else, to a breakdown in human authority needed to build and sustain healthy school cultures. Educators feel powerless to act on their best judgment, much less build a culture of excellence and caring. Teachers and principals struggle to make a difference in a toxic atmosphere of disorder, disrespect, and entitlements. This futility infects students and parents, imparting a sense of fatalism instead of hope.

The breakdown of authority has two main causes: an accretion of government mandates that has progressively narrowed the range for professional autonomy, and union collective bargaining controls that undermine principals' authority.

Since collective bargaining was authorized in the late 1960s, union leaders and officials have engaged in a kind of competition for control of schools, with each imposing more mandates and restrictions to keep the other in check. What's left is a tangle of exposed legal wires that, at any moment, could inflict shocks on a teacher or principal. This is a reason bad schools generally have cultures of fear and distrust and why many schools more closely resemble penal institutions than centers to nurture the skills and values of the next generation.

Once regulatory and union dictates have corroded school cultures, it is no longer sufficient to remove those controls. Achieving mutual trust is almost impossible in an organization that is permeated with distrust. What's generally required is either powerful leadership or a new institution where ground rules are set on day one and enforced.

I make this argument not as a policy preference, but as an immutable organizational imperative. Reempowering professional authority must be the North Star of school reform for these reasons:

1. There is no such thing as a good school without a good culture.

2. Good cultures in turn are impossible unless teachers have agency—specifically, the authority to draw on their perceptions and personalities when interacting with students, parents, and other teachers. Teachers must feel the pride of making a difference.

3. Setting and enforcing standards and values is essential to mutual trust and commitment. This is the job of principals and school leaders. Without their authority, school cultures erode.

4. Fixing America's schools is impossible until we reempower educators to make these daily choices.

Why Authority in Schools Is Essential

To the modern mind, restoring authority seems like an invitation for arbitrary or abusive decisions. Central mandates are aimed at precluding any neglect or error. Teachers unions justify multi-hundred-page collective bargaining agreements as protection against unfair authority: It's simply a protection of teachers' rights, unions argue. Rights against what? Against management decisions by people in charge.

This conventional wisdom is backwards—without authority, everyone within an institution loses freedom. Disorder replaces order. Defensiveness replaces confidence that everyone will be held to the same standards. Discouragement replaces pride in the common mission.

The authority of school leaders to uphold standards and cultural values instills mutual trust and provides a framework that empowers teachers to channel their energy towards engaging student learning. Authority can be abused, but responsible authority is essential to instilling a cooperative culture and confidence that all are rowing together.[1]

Organizational protocols in schools, such as pedagogy, testing, and declarations of moral principles, are not sufficient to build a successful school culture. School values only come to life in countless daily interactions. Effective teaching hinges on the personality of the teacher. Maintaining standards hinges on judgments by the school principal. Decisions on the spot—what's fair and what's not, what trade-offs are needed—are what determines the culture. That's why good schools are hard to replicate.

The disempowerment of school leaders in the last fifty years is the main reason bad schools get worse, and why mediocre schools rarely improve. Bureaucratic and union controls have usurped the human authority to make the everyday choices needed to build and support effective schools.

The Litmus Test: School Culture

The human dimension of schools is often overlooked in reform efforts. Walking into a school, experts say, they can tell in five minutes whether the school is successful. The culture emits a kind of hum; students and teachers seem to have a sense of purpose and appear direct and respectful in their interactions.[2] Schools with such cultures almost always have superior academic performance, and, even more important, impart constructive lifelong habits.[3]

A culture represents an amalgam of shared values and habits—an invisible structure that instills trust in mutual goals and obligations and restrains antisocial behavior. Common components of a good school culture include order, a disciplined approach to the common mission of learning, and mutual respect. School cultures are activated by continual choices in interactions among teachers and students and others. Teachers have agency. Students feel known. Parents understand they can make a difference.

People are not widgets, and healthy school cultures foster pride and responsibility by honoring human individuality within the framework of common values. What do you think? Why do you seem upset today? Is this student lagging behind? If so, let's give extra help.

Teachers and students feel not like isolated atoms, but like part of a cultural fabric of cooperation in which the school is far stronger than the sum of its parts.

Probably the best test of a healthy school culture is how people feel about it. When observing an inspiring teacher, Philip Jackson and his co-authors of *The Moral Life of Schools* noted that "the most important thing" she communicates is that she "likes being where she is and doing what she's doing."[4] A principal of a successful public school in Tallahassee put it this way: "Remember, classrooms are most effective when students have strong feelings about their teachers. It's the engagement!"[5]

Contrary to Tolstoy's maxim about happy families (all the same) and unhappy families (unhappy in different ways), education expert Frederick Hess posits that all good schools are unique.[6]

Good schools differ widely in their cultural personalities. They can be disciplinarian (think of Joe Clark walking the halls with a baseball bat), achievement-focused (such as Eva Moskowitz's Success Academy), values-focused (such as Knowledge Is Power Program [KIPP] schools' early motto: "Work Hard. Be Nice."), subject matter focused (for example, the maritime, environmental, and social justice high schools sponsored by Urban Assembly in New York), organized around student collaboration and learning pods instead of front-of-classroom teaching, or religious-focused (parochial and sectarian schools).

Good school cultures also have very different organizational structures. KIPP schools give teachers substantial freedoms to adapt and supplement the curriculum, whereas Success Academy has a seamless curriculum grade by grade. Success Academy's curriculum conformity, which allows students to have a common base of knowledge as they move from grade to grade, would not work in schools with students reading at dramatically different grade levels.

Other organizational features of Success Academy that help build its culture include these:

- Extracurriculars: Success offers a rich array of music, art, chess, and sports activities as a key element to instill in students a passion for life's possibilities. It marshals the resources to pay for these with larger class sizes that are generally about 20 percent larger than in public schools.

- Success Academy has an almost obsessive insistence on keeping schools and classrooms clean and in working order to avoid any impression that the school doesn't care.

- Good citizenship is part of the program. First-grade classrooms have a "job board" assigning responsibilities to hand out snacks, or be a "line leader," or a "clean-up czar." Parents too are part of the program, kept up-to-date on their children's success or challenges and invited to visit any time without prior notice.

These organizational features at Success Academy are factors in its achievement, but what brings the culture to life, Moskowitz says, are the daily choices of all the teachers and professionals in the school. It is their choices, concerns, and reactions that "make students feel loved and known for who they are" and create "a level of trust that adults in the school have their best interests at heart." "There's no getting around the judgment on the ground in classroom decision-making," Moskowitz says. "You can't script the magic of a good classroom."[7]

This is a common thread of good school cultures: teachers feel in charge of the classroom. "We have a great deal of freedom here," observed a teacher at a successful public school studied by Sara Lawrence-Lightfoot, because the principal "protects his faculty from 'the arbitrary regulations of the central authority.'"[8]

A profile of Deborah Kenny, head of Harlem Village Academies, concluded that "her staff exudes a kind of joi de education—many had taught in schools where bureaucratic malaise stifled their ambitions. Kenny gives them a remarkable amount of freedom. . . . She wants her staff to shine as brightly as her pupils."[9] Kenny attributes her success to "one core idea: belief in the power of teachers."[10] "The solution is . . . giving teachers choice, freedom, support and respect. And then holding them accountable for results."[11]

Good school cultures tend to be self-perpetuating. Once their values take hold, they guide new teachers and students as long as people in charge do not tolerate transgressions. Successful schools keep being successful.

Organizing Schools to Fail

Failing schools generally continue to fail. A low-performing work culture will breed low expectations and cynicism, and failure becomes self-fulfilling.

Frederick Hess observes that, unlike the unique personalities of good schools, "there's a kind of dreary uniformity" to bad schools: "Classrooms manage to be both disorganized and oddly rote. . . . Lessons are lackluster and the air reeks of lifeless obligation. Classrooms may be chaotic or they may be passive, but they're consistently devoid of wonder or passion."[12]

Mediocre schools are the norm in America, at least as measured by academic achievement. Although spending almost 40 percent more per student, America ranks below average among Organisation for Economic Co-operation and Development (OECD) countries in mathematics, and modestly above average in science and reading.[13] The middling rankings actually understate their poor performance:

- National averages, however low, obscure the fact that many inner-city schools teach almost nothing—they are more like holding pens for minority youth. In forty-five schools in Chicago in 2023, not one student was proficient in reading or math.[14] In New Orleans before Hurricane Katrina, students who graduated with As couldn't write a complete sentence. The valedictorian at one high school couldn't graduate because she failed the state graduation proficiency test—despite taking it five times.[15]

- In schools with mediocre or better achievement, the main determinant of performance is family income and education, not school competence.[16]

Scores have been dropping since 2012, a trend that was accelerated by COVID-19.[17] Stopping this decline seems beyond anyone's power.

The theme that runs through countless studies and reports on America's schools is a pervasive sense of powerlessness.[18] Teachers and principals feel like workers on a bureaucratic assembly line—as one teacher put it, "I'm being forced to function as a cog in a wheel and this wheel is not turning in the right direction."[19]

The idea of centralized control over schools goes back to Horace Mann in the mid-nineteenth century, but the accretion of mandates and controls since the 1960s has put educators in a kind of legal stranglehold.[20] These legal controls, in roughly chronological order: (1) gave teachers unions collective bargaining power over school decisions;[21] (2) gave students legal rights to dispute disciplinary decisions;[22] (3) created a separate framework of rights and obligations for special needs students;[23] (4) imposed ever more mandates and reporting requirements for curriculum, discipline, truancy, testing, diversity, permissible books, and anything else legislators could think of;[24] and (5) layered on top of all this a heavy federal blanket of penalties and incentives, notably No Child Left Behind in 2001 and Race to the Top in 2009.

For decades, state legislatures and school boards have been imposing ever more mandates—in some states, literally thousands of requirements. California, for example, has 746 pages of requirements on sex education.[25] New York State has mandates to teach about the Irish Potato Famine and to measure students' body mass index.[26] Recent changes to Florida law have some districts requiring written permission before distributing a Band-Aid.[27] I once saw a New York City handbook on students' rights that was 200 pages long.

Trying to teach while complying with reams of mandates causes cognitive overload, and makes teachers burn out. The most cited reason good teachers quit, according to a 2007 California study, is frustration with bureaucracy. "There is no rhyme or reason for many things we are asked to do," said one teacher in the survey who quit after eight years because of the "wasted time and energy" caused by "many silly procedures."[28]

The main job of principals and other school leaders is compliance and documentation, not leadership. Frederick Hess describes a Nevada evaluation mandate for a "sixteen-plus-page evaluation for every single teacher, with dozens of indicators that each required multiple 'pieces of evidence' . . . [consuming] more than three hours writing . . . beyond the observation, note-taking, and debrief time." An analysis calculated that these write-ups consume nineteen eight-hour days per year for each principal.[29]

Former teacher and Rhode Island education commissioner Ken Wagner observed that "new teachers come into schools like candles. Then the system starts snuffing them out." Wagner recites a litany of requirements that prevent them from dealing with the situation at hand: Follow the lesson plan. Focus on standardized tests. No exceptions for that student. No, we can't fix the water leak. Prove in a legal hearing that the student was disruptive. Ignore the parents. Don't even think about being creative. Stay within the boundaries of the union contract. "After five or ten years, many teachers have had their spirit squeezed out of them. What's left are a few heroes in an impossible system."[30]

Abolish Most Controls: Bureaucracy Can't Teach

Looking back at fifty years of reforms, it seems that political leaders mistook oversight of schools as regulatory activity. The giant school bureaucracy is aimed not at success, but at avoiding any possible error.

A kind of control mania consumes legislatures, school boards, and teachers unions. Like quarreling puppet masters, politicians and union leaders negotiate for ever more controls, largely oblivious to the effects on real people at the end of their legal strings. Principals and teachers are jerked here and there by mandates and controls that prevent them from building healthy school cultures.

Controls on schools have replaced the human authority needed to make them work—like "farming on concrete," as one educator told public management guru David Osborne.[31]

Controls to prevent unfairness have instead precluded fairness—disruptive students run amok and ineffective teachers stay on the job. Controls mandating gold-plated services for one activity or group—say, special-needs students—use up resources for others. Controls on what to teach preclude other important topics. Controls mandating compliance and reporting consume time and resources now no longer available for teaching.[32]

Almost all these bureaucratic controls must be purged. State by state, governors should appoint spring cleaning commissions to evaluate bureaucratic overload and recommend simple frameworks that set goals, allocate authority, and provide a hierarchy of accountability. In general, public schools should have similar freedoms as charter schools.

The replacement for red tape is accountability. Who decides that? Principals should presumptively make those decisions. To overcome the deep distrust that permeates schools, there should be a safeguard against arbitrary choices—for example, giving a parent-teacher committee authority to veto termination decisions. But any such reviews must be based on human judgment, not legal proof. The judgments and values required to build and maintain a good school culture cannot be demonstrated in a legal trial.

The main role of political authority over schools should be to evaluate and replace school leaders who are not effective—not manage schools with distant dictates. Instilling confidence in those decisions is probably best accomplished by outside evaluations of schools that include surveys and interviews with all stakeholders. Such reviews can give a fuller picture of school culture than merely looking at test scores or other metrics.

Beyond the red tape, what's blocking the door to a good school culture is a huge elephant: the teachers unions.

Break the Union Stranglehold

Teachers unions have an effective veto over decisions by school leaders. The most critical management choices, such as accountability, are so impractical as to be nonexistent. Collective bargaining agreements preclude choices that are standard in charter schools and require negotiating with the union rep on basic decisions on matters such as who teaches what, whether a principal can come observe a classroom, and giving a teacher special training.[33]

The corrosive effects of union contracts on school performance and culture are irrefutable, as demonstrated in studies by Terry Moe, Daniel DiSalvo, Michael Hartney, and others.[34] Near-zero accountability is a culture killer: mutual trust and pride are impossible to achieve when everyone knows performance doesn't matter.

Unions aim at protecting teachers, not schools or students. That's reason enough to remove union controls: the public purpose of schools is to prepare America's youth for productive lives in a competitive world, not provide a sinecure for teachers. But unions have done something far more insidious: they have spawned an anticulture of selfishness and entitlement:

- Harming student learning is the direct consequence of union entitlements. Exhibit A was the teachers' refusal to come back to work for almost two years during COVID, causing irreparable learning loss to millions of students. The focus of union agreements is on limiting teacher obligations, with generous sick leave and rigid collars on teaching time and interaction with the principal. In Seattle, teachers were found to have a regular practice of taking sick days on Fridays, saddling students with substitute teachers who have little idea of what students are working on.[35]

- Going the extra mile to help students is discouraged, a Johns Hopkins study found, because it "makes everyone look bad. . . . 'Unions discriminate against hard work. They put pressure on those who go above the bare minimum.'"[36] A young teacher in Boston was dressed down by a union rep after she volunteered to help out with breakfast duty for students from poor families: "There is no breakfast duty. In the last contract, it didn't come up. We didn't negotiate it. There IS NO breakfast duty. I don't care who wants to do it, there is no breakfast duty."[37]

- Teachers unions see their job as defending "teachers who shouldn't even be pumping gas."[38] Hiring teachers based on quality is precluded by seniority rights. Indeed, unions go out of their way to make sure excellent teachers are laid off first if they lack seniority, including "teachers of the year" in California and Minnesota.[39]

The fig leaf that the union elephant tries to hide behind is due process. Don't teachers deserve due process? What if a principal is unfair?

But unfair to whom? The union's myopic view of individual rights ignores the rights of students or other teachers. What about the rights of students stuck in a classroom with an inept or uncaring teacher?

Americans are conditioned to assume that any choice that adversely affects someone must be provable. But how does a principal prove which teacher is ineffective, or bores students, or is uncaring? Hearings to terminate poor teachers are exercises of legal sophistry—in one case, turning on whether the school could produce "evidence" proving that the teacher had a duty to grade papers.[40] What unions mean by due process is entitlement to the job, no matter how terrible the teacher. The proof is in the pudding: a study in Illinois found that, over an eighteen-year period, an average of two out of ninety-five thousand teachers were terminated for performance.[41]

Fairness is important to a healthy school culture. But fairness requires judgment, not proof. Here is what the head of a charter school told me about why the school terminated a teacher who, on paper, should have been perfect:

> We had a teacher here—a really nice guy with great credentials and several years of teaching under his belt—who just couldn't relate to the students. It's hard to put my fingers on exactly why. He would blow a little hot and cold, letting one student get away with talking in class and then coming down hard on someone else who did the same thing. . . . But the effect was that kids started arguing back. It affected the whole school. Kids would come out of his

class in a belligerent mood. . . . We worked with him on classroom management the summer after his first year. It usually helps, but he just didn't have the knack. So we had to let him go.[42]

Making the choices to build and sustain a healthy school culture is *the job of principals*, not an abuse of state power. Nor, as noted above, is it hard to require a second opinion or approval to protect against an arbitrary or abusive termination—as when some large employers solicit the opinions of co-workers before terminating someone.[43] But imposing a requirement of legal proof on principals is tantamount to removing their authority.

Teachers unions are accepted as a state of nature, like an unavoidable evil. But, as I explain in *Not Accountable*, public unions are different in kind from private trade unions—they have no market constraints, and represent a delegation of governing power to a private party, contrary to basic principles of constitutional governance.[44] Teachers union powers were granted as a side effect of the 1960s rights revolution, and have evolved in ways that would shock the original proponents of public unionization.

A political remedy to union power is unrealistic. That's because teachers union political power is preemptive: In thirty-six states, Terry Moe found, teachers union political contributions exceeded *all business groups combined.*[45] Public unions have, in effect, consolidated the massive size of modern government as a political force to prevent the reform of government.

Throwing off union controls requires a constitutional challenge. Voters elect reform-minded mayors who come to office shackled by preexisting collective bargaining agreements. Governing power has been delegated to private parties, contrary to core constitutional principles of nondelegation.[46] How can democracy work if the people elected to operate government have no authority over public operations?

One untapped ally for challenging union controls is the teachers themselves. Union contracts deprofessionalize teachers, treating them like workers on an assembly line. Teacher quality is irrelevant: teacher pay, assignments, and layoffs are determined by seniority. Good new ideas are foreclosed by the contract. Under union contracts, the job of the teacher requires little more than going through the motions, which eventually poisons the spirit of the most idealistic teachers. Teachers in private schools, by contrast, have higher levels of job satisfaction despite earning materially less.[47]

To fix America's schools, this battle against union control must be won. American voters today elect mayors and governors who, under union agreements, have no authority to overhaul bad schools.[48]

Acknowledging System Failure: Time to Push the Reset Button

American schools have been organized "on the totally erroneous assumption," management expert Peter Drucker observed, "that there is one right way to learn and it is the same for everyone."[49]

America's schools are treated today like other arms of government. But most governing responsibilities are regulatory or reactive to possible violations of law, and are governed by laws and regulations that are supposed to be uniform and generally centralized.[50]

Schools are different from governing. There's no reason for schools to be uniform, and, as discussed, uniformity tends to destroy their spirit. Schools are supposed to provide the training and values for individuals to flourish, not to extrude them through a common mold. It's hard to imagine a worse structure than one that organizes schools like a police function, handcuffing teachers and principals. Just as the country can't flourish with decrepit infrastructure, so too it can't flourish with schools that are organized with one-size-fits-all codebooks. Another harm of dreary public schools is the creation of a two-tier society—one in which about 17 percent of students get a chance at excellent education in private and charter schools, and most other students get the educational dregs.[51]

The idea of centralized controls was championed for business efficiency by Frederick Winslow Taylor's ideas of "scientific management."[52] But large companies are discovering that centralized control systems—such as fifty thousand "key performance indicators" at software company SAP—are inefficient and skew incentives away from responsible decisions.[53]

The vitality of organizational cultures, management expert Michele Zanini has concluded, requires a sense of ownership in the institution's values by the people doing the work. Especially for service providers, local autonomy improves customer and employee satisfaction while dramatically reducing overhead—examples include a Dutch home healthcare company that is organized into twelve-person pods and a Swedish bank that gives autonomy to each branch.[54] Large manufacturers such as Toyota, Michelin, steelmaker Nucor, and appliance giant Haier are organized to empower the judgment of employees at all levels of responsibility, including on the assembly line.[55]

Even regulators are starting to discover that allowing regulated entities to use their common sense in meeting regulatory goals results in better outcomes than rigid rules and formal procedures. The quality of nursing homes in Australia dramatically improved when it replaced prescriptive rulebooks with thirty-one general principles—for example, to provide a "homelike environment." Instead of trudging through red tape, all participants could focus on the residents' needs.

Accountability was for overall quality of the nursing home, not rote rule compliance and correct paperwork.[56]

Empowering people on the ground does not mean anything goes. There's still an important role for protocols in any organization, but those structures should be adapted to the needs of each school and directed at enhancing the ability to deliver the goals, not at control for its own sake. For example, the "job board" in the first-grade classroom at Success Academy is an educational tool that inculcates a sense of citizenship. Success Academy protocols engaging parents are aimed at enlisting them in the educational progress of their children since, as education expert Paul Hill told me, "The most important teachers are the parents."[57]

As with Australia's nursing homes, and with the companies described above, clear-cutting red tape will liberate teachers and principals to focus on students, and unlock resources for better salaries and services. It will also go a long way towards rejuvenating teaching as an honored profession.

The Cure to Bad Schools: Build New Schools

Successful schools generally fall into two categories: schools with a tradition of excellence, and new schools started from scratch, such as KIPP and Success Academy.

Fixing a bad school culture is so difficult that the best strategy is generally to close them and start over.[58] The culture of poor schools is permeated with too many antisocial habits and values, and too much distrust. Getting everyone to believe in a new mission, and in each other, is like putting fumes back into a bottle.

There are examples of turnarounds of mediocre or sluggish schools, but only with powerful leadership and breaking of many eggs.[59] The imminent prospect of being shut down is the one sanction of No Child Left Behind that produced significant change in poorly performing schools.[60] Turnarounds almost always involve high turnover. Teachers who resist the new values must be let go. When leading a dramatic overhaul of one of New York City's school districts in the 1980s, Anthony Alvarado is said to have caused turnover of principals and teachers of about 40 percent.[61]

New schools should be built community by community and should be free to design their own learning frameworks and cultures. There is no ideal system. In *Pluralism and American Public Education*, Ashley Rogers Berner shows that distinct approaches and cultures "offer educational advantages deriving from their clarity of focus."[62] The process of inventing a school culture is much of what will engage people to make it succeed. Opening the school door wide to the ideas and inspiration of principals, teachers, and parents will energize schools and the community at large. Instead of being organized as lackluster municipal bureaucracies, run by rote, schools will reflect the aspirations and personalities of the community.

The transformation of New Orleans schools after Hurricane Katrina demonstrates what is possible when communities can start over—after the public school system was replaced by independent charter schools, high school graduation rates improved from 52 to 72 percent, and gaps between racial groups narrowed.[63] Not all the new schools were successful—about a quarter were shuttered for poor performance.[64] But the ones that survived produced materially superior results with far better school cultures.

The secret to success of new schools in New Orleans was not educational genius or even better people, David Osborne describes, but simply the authority to make basic choices. New schools worked because, according to one school leader, "teachers and school leaders have more autonomy to be adaptive in the new system—they can improve more quickly, they can more easily make the small changes and decisions that need to be made every week and every year to better meet the needs of students and parents and teachers."[65]

Closing and rebuilding schools and empowering educators does not resolve all the challenges in American education. Teachers need more support and, in many communities, more pay. Mental health is a crisis in some schools. Many mothers and infants in poor communities need daylong programs so that the youngest children have exposure to words and stimuli essential for cognitive development.

But no meaningful progress can occur until political and educational leaders acknowledge that the bureaucratic model of America's public schools has failed. The control model fails because it crushes the human spirit and autonomy needed to build and sustain good school cultures. Those top-down frameworks should be abandoned, and communities empowered to rebuild America's schools as local institutions rooted in local values and personalities.

ESCAPE FROM QUICKSAND
A NEW FRAMEWORK FOR MODERNIZING AMERICA

In the 2021 Infrastructure Investment and Jobs Act, $7.5 billion was allocated to build out a national network of electric vehicle charging stations. By July 2024, three years later, eleven charging stations had been built.[1] The same act allocated $42.5 billion to expand broadband coverage to "unserved" areas. By the end of 2024, no services had been provided.[2] This is a pattern. In 2009, Congress allocated $5 billion to weatherproof older homes, estimating that 2,500 homes per month would be fixed in California alone. At the end of 2009, the total number of homes weatherproofed in California was twelve.[3]

Modernizing America's infrastructure is universally recognized as a vital national goal. Massive appropriations and ample private capital are waiting on the sidelines. But not much gets built.

Most observers, including myself, have fingered labyrinthian permitting processes, often involving state and local approvals as well as federal approvals. But the culprit is not just lengthy processes: Multiple mandates by federal, state, and local agencies often preclude officials from weighing costs and benefits sensibly, and provide serial veto points for opponents to challenge projects. There's also now a flaw in America's public culture: Officials see their job as caretakers to these processes, not decision-makers. Giving and exercising the authority to make ultimate decisions is considered dangerous, even illegal.

Saying "Go" to infrastructure requires a value judgment about trade-offs. Every project causes environmental harm of some sort—transmission lines and wind turbines defile the natural landscape, offshore platforms disturb the seabed and risk significant environmental damage if they fail, mines destroy land and pollute wherever tailings are stored, and so forth. These trade-offs rarely have a "correct" answer. What is the "correct" amount of degradation of a seaside vista to allow in exchange for offshore wind energy generation? These choices are ultimately political in character.

Environmentalists and officials are suffering from what environmentalist Michael Gerrard calls "tradeoff denial"[4]—striving to mollify every objector while refusing to recognize the far greater environmental costs of delay.

They've sunk into a kind of regulatory quicksand, flailing in rules, processes, and legal challenges, without any line of sight to the public goal. Years go by as experts discuss the minutiae of each objection. Courts then repeat the scrutiny. Cutting short these processes is like violating a religious ritual. In the temple of environmental scrutiny, mandarins with graduate degrees analyze each objection, striving for a result that achieves one best result. No pebble is left unturned.

Even the president feels powerless to interfere. President Obama, for example, sold the $800 billion 2009 stimulus package as a way to modernize infrastructure: "I think we can get a lot of work done fast." But then he discovered that "there's no such thing as shovel-ready projects."[5]

The failure of the 2009 stimulus to jumpstart infrastructure spending highlighted the need to shorten the processes that must be exhausted before anyone breaks ground. In a 2015 white paper for Common Good, "Two Years, Not Ten Years," we calculated that delays commonly double or triple the effective cost of infrastructure.[6] We also found that lengthy environmental reviews often cause dramatic environmental harm—prolonging polluting bottlenecks and delaying access to sustainable energy.

In December 2015, President Obama signed the FAST (Fixing America's Surface Transportation) Act, designed to consolidate road and rail approvals and move projects along.[7] It sought to reduce duplicative reviews, created a public dashboard for following the intricate steps in the process, and formed a sixteen-agency Federal Permitting Steering Council to coordinate agencies and resolve disagreements among them. The FAST Act, proponents claimed, would "improve the federal permitting process to promote expansion [and] economic growth."[8]

A few months later, I was summoned to a meeting of the White House Council on Environmental Quality, where twenty or so officials explained to me how the FAST Act was resolving the delays. I had a question: If one or more of the sixteen agencies don't agree, who has authority to make a decision? The response was immediate: "Oh, no one has that authority. That would be too dangerous."

Herein lies the nub of the problem. Only people, not processes, can make the decisions needed to govern. The year before the FAST Act was passed, the average time to complete an environmental impact statement (EIS) was 4.7 years. Four years later, in 2019, the average time to complete an EIS was . . . 4.7 years.[9]

Additional reforms in 2021 and 2023 contained a number of changes recommended in "Two Years, Not Ten Years," such as page limits on environmental reviews, time limits for approval, the designation of one lead agency, shorter statutes of limitations for court challenges, and limiting agency analysis to only "reasonably foreseeable" impacts.[10]

Early indications suggest that these reforms have not worked—for example, the three-year lag (so far) in building electric charging stations. Better process is no cure for a system that sees process as an end in itself. There is always another objection and something else to study. The time and page limits get stuck in the muck of countless competing regulatory requirements.

Modernizing infrastructure—indeed, reforming government to work sensibly in almost every area—requires a new framework based on a different operating philosophy. Public choices should be made by officials who are accountable, not by navigating a legal labyrinth. Instead of cutting red tape here and there, reform must start with defining official authority to make ultimate decisions. Processes and regulations should then be remade to set goals, guiding principles, and lines of accountability within which these designated officials are allowed to act.

In November 1933, FDR created the Civil Works Administration (CWA) to give jobs to the unemployed and put Harry Hopkins in charge. By the end of December, less than two months later, more than 2 million Americans had been hired by CWA.[11] What would FDR have done if he had been told that there were "no shovel-ready projects"? A day or so later, Congress likely would have been presented a short bill authorizing the executive branch to fund any projects deemed in the public interest.

The governing philosophy of the New Deal was to give officials "grants of power with which to act decisively."[12] The New Deal projects worked not only because officials had the legal authority to push ambitious projects forward, but also because those officials viewed their responsibility as achieving results.

Laws don't govern. People do. Laws are supposed to provide the framework within which elected and appointed officials have room to make the decisions needed for the public good. "It is one of the most prominent features of the constitution, a principle that pervades the whole system," as James Madison explained, "that there should be the highest possible degree of responsibility in all the Executive officers thereof."[13]

Today, the focus on process and compliance has fostered an official culture of avoiding decisions. Taking clippers to the current thicket can never work, because what's left is designed to supplant human judgment. Years go by and costs multiply as officials neglect the public good in the pursuit of legal compliance.

How Process Replaced Good Government

The utility of environmental review, mandated by the National Environmental Policy Act of 1970 (NEPA),[14] is broadly accepted. The idea is to inform official decisions by presenting benefits and harms of proposed projects and to promote political accountability through greater transparency. NEPA's legislative sponsors thought that reviews would be a few dozen pages in length and be completed in a matter of months.[15] The act provided no right to judicial review.

But judicial activism was in vogue in the 1970s, and federal courts demanded that agencies take a "hard look" at environmental impacts.[16] The "hard look" doctrine allowed courts to reject any project with which they disagreed. Under the guise of requiring further analysis, courts signal to agencies that a different judgment is needed to pass judicial muster.

Courts ostensibly are mandating compliance with NEPA. But environmental review is different from, say, fire and safety codes. A safety regulation has a clear purpose and leaves only a narrow scope for official interpretation. Disclosure of environmental effects and alternatives, by contrast, is open-ended. There's always something else to study. Whatever strikes the court as harmful can be sent back for further review.

In the name of better disclosure, courts undermined the authority of the executive branch. The ability of an official to act on his or her best judgment was replaced by a court demanding that officials must demonstrate the correctness of their judgments.

Congress and state legislatures piled on by enacting laws to protect this or that. Modern government is organized into scores of discrete silos overseeing emissions, fish and wildlife, wetlands, deserts, historic buildings, public lands, tribal lands, civil rights, and so forth. The laws enacting these regulations sometimes require that environmental reviews specify how projects "minimize the impact" on, say, historic buildings or endangered species—putting the thumb on the scale for those goals over others and disregarding the reality that public goals are often in conflict.[17]

Public transparency—the main goal of NEPA—has been drowned in a tsunami of often unintelligible detail. The project to raise the roadway of the Bayonne Bridge over the entrance to Newark Harbor, for example, would allow for the passage of the new generation of post-Panamax ships, which are more efficient as well as greener. Raising the roadway had minimal environmental impact because it used the same foundations and rights-of-way. The permit was granted—but only after five years and an environmental assessment of 20,000 pages, including exhibits.

You might wonder what possibly was in all that material. Though the project affected no buildings, a state mandate required the sponsor to study the impact on historic buildings within a two-mile radius. It also had to solicit input from Native American tribes around the country whose ancestors might once have lived on the land.

Then came the litigation. An environmental group challenged the project on the grounds that the 20,000-page assessment was inadequate. But, as in many of these situations, the objectors were not really interested in more disclosure. It turned out that the challenge was funded by the Teamsters union, which hoped to use the delay of litigation as a lever to make the Port Authority agree to ban independent truckers.[18]

On average, as noted, federal environmental approval takes over four years.[19] Lawsuits challenging review on large projects consume another 3½–4½ years.[20] Important projects—such as transmission lines over new rights-of-way, or urban projects that affect a neighborhood, or disturbing a natural habitat—often take much longer. A permit to dredge the Savannah River took sixteen years.[21] Paralysis by analysis leads to many projects being abandoned, such as controlled burns in California to deter fires.[22]

Despite recent reforms that limit the time for permitting and size of review documents, courts continue to see their job as scrutinizing the completeness of disclosure. In 2024, the D.C. Circuit Court of Appeals blocked a liquefied natural gas facility on the basis that the environmental review did not sufficiently study the "environmental justice" of a facility located near a low-income neighborhood.[23] Another court blocked offshore drilling in the Gulf of Mexico because the effects on Rice's whales were insufficiently studied.[24]

How Process Became Quicksand: The Microeconomics of Avoiding Human Judgment

The premise of the "legal process" movement that

remade public decision-making in the 1960s was that officials should not assert "final answers" but oversee a process that is "content neutral" and provides "an agreeable procedure for getting acceptable answers."[25] All the information piles up, interested parties make their arguments, and eventually some version of the project gets a green light.

Without human responsibility linked to actual results, however, this process guarantees failure. That's because facts and arguments don't automatically congeal into a decision.[26] There's always an argument for a different result. Agencies with conflicting priorities will argue for a different analysis. Motivated interest groups will press hard for their position.[27] Officials in charge find themselves in a defensive posture, knowing that their decisions will be reviewed by a court. They focus not on making the best decision but a decision that minimizes the chance of reversal.

When officials lack authority to act in the public interest, decisions that emerge from the process will usually undermine the public interest. *New York Times* columnist Ezra Klein decided to look into why a small public toilet in San Francisco—which cost only about $200,000—was budgeted to cost $1.7 million. The answer was layers of process and approvals:

> There's the planning and design phase, which requires bringing the design for the public toilet to "community engagement stakeholders"

and refining it based on their feedback. That typically takes three to six months. Then the Public Works Department can solicit bids from outside contractors. That takes six months. Construction takes four to six months more, depending on whether a prefab toilet is used or one is constructed on site. The toilet also needed approval from the Department of Public Works, the Planning Department, the Department of Building Inspection, the Arts Commission, the Public Utilities Commission, the Mayor's Office on Disability and PG&E, the local electric utility.[28]

Instead of a mechanism for better public choices, process itself becomes the goal. Jennifer Pahlka from the Niskanen Center describes the numerous sub-procedures that Congress and agencies have imposed. As one official summarized it: "Congress tells us to do something by a deadline. The compliance offices stop us from doing it." Processes work like tripwires, not a hierarchy for achieving goals:

> They start to hire a team, but the Office of Personnel Management tells them they've used the wrong authorities, or used them incorrectly, and they need to start over. They need to collect information from grant applicants, but the Paperwork Reduction Act review process takes an average of nine months. They need to hire a

firm to build an online application, but it will take far longer to get to a contract than it will for the firm to build the form.[29]

Almost every choice and sub-choice has its own process—not only to decide what environmental effects to study but to resolve disagreements among agencies, to keep to deadlines, to decide which consultants to hire, and to weigh benefits and costs for the ultimate decision. After the project is approved, the processes start all over again with contracting procedures.

The result is a parody of inept government. Officials are like Charlie Chaplin characters, taking this step and that, constantly diverted from acting by one more requirement: But have you studied that? Can you demonstrate that your decision wasn't motivated by favoritism or bias? How does the association of birdwatchers feel about it?

Why do we accept this failed system? On some deep level, we no longer believe in human judgment. Pahlka sees the "fetishization of process as a sort of talisman" that verifies officials' virtue.[30] "Strict adherence to a process" means that "no judgment can be questioned, because no judgment was used."[31] In his study of federal procurement, public-management scholar Steven Kelman describes a public culture that has been brainwashed: "Our system for managing in the public sector may rob the people in it of their faculties to such an extent that, like a person on a mind-numbing drug, they no longer even realize that they are missing anything."[32]

Czech statesman and philosopher Václav Havel saw the obsession with finding external justifications—rather than trusting our own judgment—as a deep insecurity of modern society that is striving for "an objective way out of a crisis of objectivism."[33] Instead of taking responsibility, we prove our virtue by refusing to take responsibility.

The compulsive drive to purge human judgment has a clear history.[34] Coming out of the upheavals of the 1960s, we wanted to create a government better than people. No more discrimination, pollution, or other abuses of authority by officials like Robert Moses. We not only came to distrust other people, particularly people with authority, but also to distrust ourselves. Who are we to judge? Every aspect of the process must be free from the taint of subjective judgments. So we cling tightly to processes that relieve us of the burden of deciding almost anything.

It's a downward spiral. Distrust of human judgment leads to disempowerment, which causes paralysis, which leads to greater failure and distrust.

Burning Money: How Procurement Processes Compound the Waste

Delays in infrastructure permitting are compounded by procurement procedures that are also designed to replace an official's judgment with neutral, objective processes. The idea is to minimize fraud or favoritism. There is hardly any action that engenders more distrust than spending public money, but, as with permitting, the procedural approach generally guarantees the waste that it seeks to prevent.

Just as permitting requires judgments about trade-offs, implementation requires making countless decisions to adapt to unforeseen circumstances and glitches. Management theorist Chester Barnard thought that "nine-tenths of all organization activity is on the responsibility, the authority . . . of those who make the last contributions, who apply personal energies to the final concrete objectives."[35]

Businesses understand the need for flexibility. That's why they contract with vendors whom they trust and, instead of specifying every detail, leave room to work out unanticipated issues. In design-build contracts, they kick all these choices on implementation to the contractor.

The public sector, by contrast, uses formalistic procurement processes aimed at purging human judgment at all steps. Detailed specifications are set forth in a "request for proposals" (RFP); then there is an advertisement for all qualified bidders; then an evaluation of bids by a mathematical formula; and then the contract is awarded to the bidder with the most points. Losing bidders can challenge the award as noncompliant with any of the formal criteria.[36]

These procurement processes generally result in worse products at higher prices, for reasons that are self-evident to any practical person:

- Specifying all details in advance consumes time and leaves no flexibility for unforeseen complications. Each change order then requires a separate process and price negotiation. Specifying details in advance also precludes the trial and error and collaborative engagement essential for most information-technology projects. Artificial intelligence cannot be developed or used effectively, for example, without ongoing exercise of human intelligence.

- Formalistic processes require bidders to raise prices to compensate for the inefficient rigidities. Building "affordable housing" in California, for example, often requires loans from multiple public programs—each with a separate contract and duplicative compliance requirements to ensure that the developer stays within rent guidelines. As a result of these and other formal requirements, the cost of an "affordable housing" apartment in California is about $750,000—about triple the cost of comparable apartments built by private developers in Dallas.[37]

- Neutrality towards bidders—meant as a check against favoritism—means that government sometimes awards bids to contractors who have performed poorly in the past. In his study of procurement, Kelman quotes an official who felt proud that he was "objective enough" to ignore that a bidder had performed poorly in previous contracts.[38]

These complexities are multiplied by other requirements aimed at pursuing collateral goals irrelevant to the completion of a project. The Biden administration's inability to expand broadband service, for example, was partly due to a tangle of requirements regarding whom should be given contracts. Implementation of the project, according to FCC commissioner Brendan Carr, was "chaotic" because "[i]nstead of focusing on delivering broadband to unserved areas, the administration has . . . adopted regulations that include diversity, equity and inclusion requirements, climate-change rules, price controls, preferences for union labor, and schemes that favor government-run networks."[39]

Apologists for the procurement process argue that inefficiency is a small price to pay to avoid favoritism and corruption. But the procedures breed a kind of corruption by interest groups who know how to play the game. Partly because labor unions successfully lobbied for procurement rules that require overstaffing, the Second Avenue subway in New York cost $2.5 billion per mile—five times the cost of a similar subway in Paris.[40]

Studies on corruption uniformly conclude that the best safeguard is not the avoidance of human responsibility but a transparent hierarchy that empowers officials and thereby creates a clear sightline of accountability.[41] The public procurement process does the opposite, obscuring accountability in a maze of procedures. The public gets worse products at higher prices, with no accountability.

The alternative way of awarding contracts is not unfettered discretion. Principles of competitive bidding are important in most circumstances. But they must ultimately be activated by responsible officials who have authority to use their judgment.

The Miracle of Letting Officials Take Responsibility

On June 11, 2023, a truck delivering 8,500 gallons of gasoline crashed underneath an elevated section of I-95 in Philadelphia and burst into flames, causing a section of the highway to collapse.[42] Initial reports suggested that traffic in the Northeast Corridor would be snarled for months. Twelve days later, the highway was reopened.

The key to the speedy repair was Pennsylvania governor Josh Shapiro's declaration of an emergency, which suspended all regulations that "would in any way prevent, hinder, or delay necessary action." Ignoring procurement rules, the state immediately hired a reputable local highway contractor to perform "extra work" on existing contracts, thus avoiding the need for competitive bids.

The quickest way to build temporary lanes on an elevated road is to pave on top of landfill, but 12,000-plus tons of dirt and rock might cause underlying water and sewer mains to collapse. Michael Carroll, head of the state's Department of Transportation, proposed using recycled glass, one-sixth the weight. Based on this quick engineering assessment, a deal was made with a nearby recycled-glass company, which started delivering recycled glass around the clock. Again, procurement rules were ignored. All these decisions also require permits from numerous state and local agencies. Carroll spent his days at the site, issuing or waiving permit requirements.

On June 23—twelve days after the accident—I-95 reopened. The quick repair was not a miracle. The people in charge simply took responsibility to get the job done, using common sense, existing commercial and community relationships, and a little creativity. "We showed . . . good government action," Governor Shapiro declared.

Governor Shapiro's quick action has been widely viewed as heroic because Americans loathe traffic jams more than they fear the exercise of executive authority.

This was an emergency, of course. But emergencies should not be the only situation where officials are allowed to use their judgment. The public good requires judgments on the trade-offs of benefits against harms, not wringing our hands over all possible harms. These choices are rarely right or wrong. Studying impacts and alternatives is useful—but only to a point.

The history of America's economic growth is highlighted by transformational public infrastructure investments:

- The Erie Canal, which New York governor DeWitt Clinton built with public funds, was a risky bet, widely derided as "Clinton's big ditch." After the canal opened in 1825, transportation costs to midwestern markets fell by 95 percent, stimulating jobs and prosperity across the Midwest and the East.[43]

- Transcontinental rail lines, built in the 1860s, were subsidized by giving railroad companies 6,400 acres of adjacent land per mile of track to entice the huge investment. These rail lines, replacing Conestoga wagons, created a national marketplace and fostered growth in areas that were little more than prairie outposts.[44]

- The Interstate Highway System, promoted by President Eisenhower as essential to national defense, was authorized in 1956 by a statute that was twenty-nine pages long.[45] A decade later, with 90 percent federal funding, over 21,000 miles had been built.[46]

None of those projects could have been built today. Would environmentalists, if given a time machine, insist on canceling them? Some could certainly have been done better—for example, avoiding interstate highways through the heart of cities. But even knowing those harms, would it have been smart to delay the Interstate Highway System for a few decades while the impacts of the first 20,000 miles were studied?

America's economy today consists of millions of moving parts that come together on the spine of our nation's infrastructure. Most of that infrastructure was built by our ancestors without the wisdom imparted by environmental review. Roads, rail, ports, power, electric lines, water, waste disposal, and other shared resources allow markets to hum, entrepreneurs to innovate, defense to mobilize, and citizens to be safe and comfortable. Those demanding a "hard look" at details of projects are doing so from the comfort of a society that never could exist on the terms they demand.

Ironically, the paralytic quest for perfect process has driven officials back to zero process as the only viable way to make timely infrastructure decisions, as with fixing I-95.[47] Broad categorical exclusions are a core feature of the pending Manchin-Barrasso bill—including exclusions from review for "low disturbance" projects, transmission lines, geothermal drilling, and more.[48]

The right balance which NEPA originally sought is one in which official choices are first exposed to public scrutiny. No one who reads *The Power Broker*, Robert Caro's magisterial biography of Robert Moses, wants to cede unilateral power to officials without public transparency. But Moses also left an astonishing legacy of exemplary public works. What's missing today is a framework that is activated by officials who take responsibility and are accountable up a political hierarchy for the results.

The Cure: A Framework with Humans in Charge

On November 15, 1933, one week after CWA was created, Harry Hopkins summoned a group of governors and mayors to discuss possible projects. On November 20, Hopkins approved 122 projects; on November 21, he approved another 109 projects, and so forth. Funds were released to local governments. Four months later, over 1,000 miles of water mains and 12 million feet of sewage pipes had been laid, 255,000 miles of roads had been paved, and numerous other public works built or improved. Auditors reviewing the projects found that, overwhelmingly, the funds had been used as intended.[49]

The solution to infrastructure paralysis is a legal framework that empowers designated officials to make multiple trade-off judgments. Choices need to be made. This requires replacing balkanized approvals by multiple agencies and multiple levels of government with one decision-making hierarchy. The designated officials and agency can differ by type of project. The deciding agency would receive input from other interested departments, but must have authority to make trade-offs that weigh benefits and harms.

This framework would be a radical simplification—replacing the labyrinth of accumulated mandates and procedures with single hierarchies, all overseen by the White House in the case of federal permits and projects. Process would be understood as a tool for making judgments, not an end in itself. Officials must be reempowered to make judgments about trade-offs at every step. A $200,000 public toilet should cost that amount, not $1.7 million.

Judgments can be made poorly, of course. That's why oversight and accountability are critical. Instead of avoiding human judgment, the checks and balances must also be built on the foundation of human judgment—giving supervisory officials the authority to oversee or approve decisions. Years of *ex ante* process can be replaced by weeks of *ex post* review.

Governing effectively is impossible until designated officials are empowered to make ultimate decisions. By contrast, reforms that strive to streamline process and cut unnecessary rules are doomed to failure—an exercise akin to trying to prune the jungle. Any disagreement among officials will cause delay, and any inconsistency among the myriad regulations will be a basis for a legal challenge.[50]

America must return to the human responsibility operating philosophy envisioned by the Framers. The current system is built on the wrong idea of law.

Law cannot make public choices. Moreover, while law can protect against arbitrary choices, it cannot validate which choice is best among a wide range of plausible options. Law instead is supposed to frame the responsibility of officials who, within legal boundaries, make choices that are politically accountable. The role of courts is not to second-guess the wisdom of these judgments but to ensure that officials do not transgress the legal boundaries—say, by conducting an environmental review so shoddy that it is arbitrary and capricious.

Three major changes are needed to restore the authority to achieve results: a new legal framework, a new institution that can inspire trust in ongoing decisions, and a special commission to design the details of these changes.

New legal framework defining official authority. Here's a sketch of what a new infrastructure decision-making framework might look like:

1. Separate agencies should be designated as decision-makers for each category of infrastructure. The head of that agency should have authority to approve permits. For federal approvals, all decisions should be subject to White House oversight. For projects with national or regional significance, federal decisions should preempt state and local approvals.

2. Fifty years of accumulated mandates from multiple agencies should be restated as public goals

that can be balanced against other public goals. As will be discussed below, a recodification commission is needed to reframe thousands of pages of detailed regulatory prescriptions into codes that are goal-oriented and honor public tradeoffs. But until this can happen, Congress should authorize the executive branch to approve permits "notwithstanding provisions of law to the contrary"—provided the executive branch identifies the relevant provisions and provides a short statement of why the approvals are in the public interest.

3. Processes should be mainly tools for transparency and should be understood by courts as general principles reviewed for abuse of discretion, not as rules requiring strict compliance. NEPA has been effectively rewritten by judicial fiat, so it should be amended to return to its original goals—to provide environmental transparency, public comment, and a political judgment.

4. The jurisdiction of courts must be sharply limited. Lawsuits should be allowed for approvals that transgress boundaries of executive responsibility, not inadequate review or process, unless these are so deficient as to be arbitrary.[51]

Changing law is always politically difficult, but the second challenge is perhaps even harder: creating new institutions that can inspire trust.

Oversight by a national infrastructure board. The public is conditioned to think the worst of officials. For officials, partisan acrimony creates powerful incentives to avoid judgment altogether—every approval has objectors, and no official wants to be put under klieg lights at a congressional committee.[52] The bureaucratic process today, with nearly endless meetings and legal bickering, operates like an invisible shield protecting officials against political backbiting.

Reinstilling officials' confidence to make decisions requires a new oversight institution that officials and the public can trust to validate permitting and contracting decisions. I propose creating an independent "national infrastructure board" to advise political leaders and the public on the priorities and progress of infrastructure projects. Just as base-closing commissions provide a foundation of moral support for difficult choices, a national infrastructure board could validate sensible trade-off judgments and defuse politically motivated attacks.[53] A critical role of a national infrastructure board would be to provide "cover" for officials who are sure to be attacked by project opponents.

Specific responsibilities of a national infrastructure board would be:

- Maintain a running list of national and regional infrastructure priorities, as a similar commission does in Australia.[54] The board could discourage wasteful projects such as the infamous "bridge to nowhere."

- Track and comment on delays in infrastructure approvals, and provide backing for projects that may be opposed by NIMBY interests.
- Oversee and certify the reasonableness of contracting procedures. Most infrastructure projects are managed by state and local governments that, as with the Second Avenue subway, have adopted wasteful procedures and work rules. The one official power that a national infrastructure board should have is to withhold infrastructure funds from project sponsors that do not conform to commercially reasonable contracting practices.

A nonpartisan recodification commission. The third and final step in this reform is to create a credible recodification committee or commission to design and propose the details of these reforms. Changes this dramatic are unlikely to emerge from backroom negotiations in Congress. There are too many conflicting interests and too much distrust.

The job of devising new simpler infrastructure codes should be delegated to a nonpartisan commission. There is a long history of recodification commissions that are charged with modernizing legal codes that have become convoluted and complex, including, for example, the creation of the Uniform Commercial Code in the 1950s.[55]

In times of war and crisis, Congress delegates the job of making decisions to small groups or commissions, as it did with the War Production Board in World War II or with Operation Warp Speed to devise COVID vaccines. In situations fraught with political conflicts, as noted above, Congress has delegated the task of making recommendations of which military bases should be closed to independent "base-closing commissions."[56]

Moral authority goes a long way towards avoiding the frictions of distrust. Members of such a recodification commission could be appointed, as with base-closing commissions: experts selected by majority and minority leaders in Congress and by the president. The special commission must make the proposal, and Congress can take it from there.

Conclusion

In June 2024, a commuter train in New York was stuck for nearly three hours in one of two Hudson River rail tunnels connecting Manhattan to all points west.[57] The tunnels were built in 1910, are in fragile condition, and provide only about half the capacity to service rail traffic in the twenty-first century. They need to be closed down to be rebuilt and hardened against events such as Superstorm Sandy, which shut them down and paralyzed commuting from New Jersey for two months in 2012.[58] Plans for new tunnels were announced beginning in 2009, but a combination of political disincentives for long-term investments and lengthy permitting deterred serious proposals.[59] In 2024, construction finally began on parts of the project. The new tunnels are expected to be in service in 2038, twenty-nine years after they were first announced.[60]

America is operating on road, rail, water, and electric infrastructure largely built by our great-grandfathers, including by Harry Hopkins's CWA. The 2025 status report by the American Society of Civil Engineers (ASCE)[61] rates American infrastructure as a C, marginally better than the C-minus from 2021,[62] but not good. The worst areas, each earning a D or D-plus, are roads, dams, levees, storm water, wastewater, schools, transit, aviation, and energy. Two additional categories of critical infrastructure are not separately rated by ASCE but deserve a poor rating: local electric distribution, which, in many places, consists of wires strung on rickety wooden power poles; and mining of rare earth and other essential metals, which is necessary to avoid dependence on China.

The social benefits of modern infrastructure are clearly visible at the end of the rainbow, if only government could make deliberate choices to move forward. High-speed transmission lines would promote more renewable power development in low-occupancy areas and also modular nuclear power. Low-lying cities would be protected from storm surges. Flexible zoning and building codes would allow new housing to sprout in underutilized urban areas. Water and wastewater distribution would be modernized. Artificial intelligence could transform public services.[63]

The economic benefits of modern infrastructure are also clear. Upgrading and expanding transmission lines alone yields a return of more than double the project costs.[64] ASCE estimates that addressing the $81 billion investment gap in water and wastewater infrastructure could save Americans almost $500 billion from decreased business disruptions, reduced waste, and improved public health.[65] They could be partly funded by user costs. America's competitiveness and security would be dramatically enhanced.

None of this can happen until the U.S. updates its legal framework to empower officials to make necessary choices. The point of environmental review should not be to avoid "subjective judgments" but to inform those judgments. The point of democracy is to elect and appoint officials to oversee and make these decisions. Without this authority, democracy can't do its job.

NOTES

Is This America's 1917 Moment?

1 Paul C. Light, "Public Demand for 'Very Major' Government Reform Is Running High," Government Executive, April 12, 2023. See also The University of Chicago, Harris School of Public Policy, "UChicago Harris/AP-NORC Poll Shows 66 Percent Think Major Structural Changes Are Needed to U.S. System of Government," May 2, 2019.

2 Vision is critical: "A building is not well erected," as Martin Luther King, Jr., told a group of students, "without a good, sound, and solid blueprint." Dr. Martin Luther King, Jr., *A Time to Break Silence: The Essential Works of Martin Luther King, Jr., for Students,* ed. Walter Dean Myers (Boston: Beacon Press, 2013), 219.

3 "There is an amazing strength," Tocqueville overserved, "in the expression of the will of a whole people." Alexis de Tocqueville, *Democracy in America*, ed. Phillips Bradley (New York: Vintage, 1990), 1:247.

4 Administrative costs account for around 30 percent of healthcare spending. See Steffie Woolhandler, MD, Terry Campbell, and David U. Himmelstein, MD, "Costs of Health Care Administration in the United States and Canada," 349 *The New England Journal of Medicine* 768 (August 2003).

5 Tocqueville, *Democracy in America*, 1:90.

6 "The difficulty lies, not in the new ideas," John Maynard Keynes observed, "but in escaping from the old ones." John Maynard Keynes, *The General Theory of Employment, Interest and Money* (New York: Harcourt, 1965), vii.

Striving: How to Recover America's Magic

1 Isaiah Berlin, *Four Essays on Liberty* (Oxford: Oxford University Press, 1969), xlix, quoting Thomas Hill Green.

2 Friedrich A. Hayek, *The Constitution of Liberty*, ed. Ronald Hamowy (Chicago: University of Chicago Press, 2011), 188: "How faithfully and intelligently . . . how well he has fitted himself into the whole machinery, must be determined by the opinion of other people."

3 **"men are never stationary"**: Alexis de Tocqueville, *Democracy in America*, ed. Phillips Bradley (New York: Vintage, 1990), 2:223.

"all-pervading and restless activity": Tocqueville, *Democracy in America*, 1:252.

4 See generally, Philip K. Howard, *Everyday Freedom: Designing the Framework for a Flourishing Society* (Garden City, NY: Rodin, 2024); Philip K. Howard, *Try Common Sense: Replacing the Failed Ideologies of Right and Left* (New York: W.W. Norton, 2019); and Philip K. Howard, *The Rule of Nobody: Saving America from Dead Laws and Broken Government* (New York: W.W. Norton, 2014).

5 Eric Foner, *The Story of American Freedom* (New York: W.W. Norton, 1998), 293.

6 **Public officials:** See generally Philip K. Howard, *Not Accountable: Rethinking the Constitutionality of Public Employee Unions* (Garden City, NY: Rodin, 2023).

Projects to modernize infrastructure: See Philip K. Howard, "Two Years, Not Ten Years: Redesigning Infrastructure Approvals," Common Good, September 2015. See also Marc J. Dunkelman, *Why Nothing Works: Who Killed Progress—and How to Bring It Back* (New York: PublicAffairs, 2025) and Ezra Klein and Derek Thompson, *Abundance* (New York: Avid Reader Press, 2025).

Candor in the workplace: See discussion in Philip K. Howard, *Life Without Lawyers: Restoring Responsibility in America* (New York: W.W. Norton, 2010), 122–49 and Philip K. Howard, *The Collapse of the Common Good: How America's Lawsuit Culture Undermines Our Freedom* (New York: Ballantine, 2001), 173–98.

Universities: See, e.g., Paul Weinstein Jr., "How to Cut Administrative Bloat at U.S. Colleges," Progressive

Policy Institute (August 2023) (describing the "significant upswing" in administrative hiring at American universities over the past two decades, driven in part by the "explosion in regulation and red tape" facing higher education) and Philip Babcock, "Real Costs of Nominal Grade Inflation? New Evidence from Student Course Evaluations," 24 *Economic Inquiry* 4 (October 2010), 983–96 (describing the "epidemic" of grade inflation in American higher education).

Failing schools: See discussion in the second essay of this book, "The Human Authority Needed for Good Schools" (originally published by Stanford University's Hoover Institution (November 2024)). See also Howard, *Not Accountable*.

The classroom: See Richard Arum, *Judging School Discipline: The Crisis of Moral Authority* (Cambridge, MA: Harvard University Press, 2005).

Parents worry: See Howard, *Life Without Lawyers*, 15–48, 68–92 and Howard, *The Collapse of the Common Good*, 3–70. See also Lenore Skenazy, *Free-Range Kids: Giving Our Children the Freedom We Had Without Going Nuts with Worry* (San Francisco: Jossey-Bass, 2009) and Jonathan Haidt, *The Anxious Generation: How the Great Rewiring of Childhood Is Causing an Epidemic of Mental Illness* (New York: Penguin, 2024), 67–94.

Managers and officials: Avoidance of candor and admonitions to watch your words are a common theme of mandatory video training.

7 Tocqueville, *Democracy in America*, 2:320.

8 Francis Hutcheson, *A Short Introduction to Moral Philosophy* (1747), republished by constitutioncenter.org. See discussion in Arthur Herman, *How the Scots Invented the Modern World: The True Story of How Western Europe's Poorest Nation Created Our World and Everything in It* (New York: Crown, 2001).

9 Tocqueville, *Democracy in America*, 2:123. See also 1:393: "They all consider society as a body in a state of improvement, humanity as a changing scene, in which nothing is, or ought to be, permanent; and they admit that what appears to them today to be good, may be superseded by something better tomorrow."

10 George Washington, Circular to the States, June 8, 1783, Founders Online (U.S. National Archives).

11 The book to read about the Wright brothers and other extraordinary stories of American initiative in commerce is *They Made America* by Harold Evans (New York: Little, Brown, 2004).

12 **"the usual process"**: Michael Polanyi, *Personal Knowledge: Towards a Post-Critical Philosophy* (Chicago: University of Chicago Press, 1962), 62.

Studies of activities: See, e.g., Mike Rose, *The Mind at Work: Valuing the Intelligence of the American Worker* (New York: Viking, 2004) and Polanyi, *Personal Knowledge*.

"disappear . . . into the task": Rose, *The Mind at Work*, 112.

Our knowledge is in our action: See Polanyi, *Personal Knowledge*, 267: "Our mind lives in action."

13 Isaiah Berlin, "Two Concepts of Liberty," from *The Proper Study of Mankind: An Anthology of Essays*, eds. Henry Hardy and Roger Hausheer (New York: Farrar, Straus and Giroux, 2000), 236.

14 Henry Steele Commager, *The American Mind: An Interpretation of American Thought and Character Since the 1880's* (New Haven, CT: Yale University Press, 1950), 363.

15 Focus on A, sociologist Robert K. Merton observed, and you do not see B. Robert K. Merton, "Bureaucratic Structure and Personality," *Social Forces* 18, no. 4 (May 1940), 562.

Working memory is tiny: See John Sweller, Paul Ayres, and Slava Kalyuga, *Cognitive Load Theory* (New York: Springer, 2011), 42–43.

"minute in its ability" and the quotations about long-term memory: John Sweller, "Evolution of Human Cognitive Architecture," in *The Psychology of Learning and Motivation*, Vol. 43, ed. Brian H. Ross (San Diego: Academic Press, 2003), 218–220.

16 See discussion of the work of psychologist John Sweller and others in Philip K. Howard, "Bureaucracy vs. Democracy: Examining the Bureaucratic Causes of Public

Failure, Economic Repression, and Voter Alienation," Columbia University Center on Capitalism and Society, Working Paper No. 113, February 4, 2019.

> **"Bureaucracy develops the more perfectly"**: Max Weber, *Economy and Society*, eds. Guenther Roth and Claus Wittich (Berkeley, CA: University of California Press, 1978), 975.
>
> **Daniel Kahneman**: See Daniel Kahneman, *Thinking, Fast and Slow* (New York: Farrar, Straus and Giroux, 2011).
>
> **William Simon**: William H. Simon, "Legality, Bureaucracy, and Class in the Welfare System," 92 *Yale Law Journal* 1198, 1198–99 (1983).

17 Arum, *Judging School Discipline*, 169.

18 John Locke, *The Second Treatise on Civil Government* (Amherst, MA: Prometheus, 1986), 33: "The end of law is not to . . . restrain, but to preserve and enlarge freedom."

19 See discussion in Howard, *The Rule of Nobody*.

20 Polanyi, *Personal Knowledge*, 79.

21 **"Good expert judgment"**: Gerd Gigerenzer, *Gut Feelings: The Intelligence of the Unconscious* (New York: Penguin, 2008), 15.

"What we reject": Philip W. Jackson, Robert E. Boostrom, and David T. Hansen, *The Moral Life of Schools* (San Francisco: Jossey-Bass, 1998), 48.

22 **"exalting what we can know and prove"**: Polanyi, *Personal Knowledge*, 286.

Government procurement: See, e.g., Steven Kelman, *Procurement and Public Management: The Fear of Discretion and the Quality of Government Performance* (Washington, DC: AEI Press, 1990), 52, and Jennifer Pahlka and Andrew Greenway, "The How We Need Now: A Capacity Agenda for 2025 and Beyond," Niskanen Center, December 2024, 24. See also discussion in the third essay of this book, "Escape from Quicksand: A New Framework for Modernizing America" (originally published by the Manhattan Institute, February 2025).

Public permitting: See, e.g., discussion of the rebuilding of the Bayonne Bridge in Howard, *The Rule of Nobody*, 7–12, 81, 160–64 and Dunkelman, *Why Nothing Works*, 280–91.

Due process hearings: Steven Brill, *Tailspin: The People and Forces Behind America's Fifty-Year Fall—and Those Fighting to Reverse It* (New York: Knopf, 2018), 265–66. See also discussion in Howard, *Not Accountable*, 53.

Broad resentment: See, e.g., John McWhorter, "Claudine Gay Was Not Driven Out Because She Is Black," *New York Times*, January 8, 2024 (claiming that DEI programs often force employers to abandon "traditional conceptions of merit [and] elevat[e] nonwhiteness as a qualification in itself," and in so doing embody an "unwitting condescension" to nonwhite applicants and employees).

23 The rejection of cultural values on the basis of their inherent subjectivity recalls what Tocqueville described as a "depraved taste for equality, which impels the weak to lower the powerful to their own level." Tocqueville, *Democracy in America*, 1:53.

24 Karol Wojtyla (Pope John Paul II), "Subjectivity and the Irreducible in the Human Being," in *Person and Community: Selected Essays* (New York: Peter Lang, 2008).

25 **"most elementary manifestation"**: Hannah Arendt, "What Is Authority?," in *The Portable Hannah Arendt* (New York: Penguin, 2003), 466.

Building trust is impossible: See Onora O'Neill, *A Question of Trust: The BBC Reith Lectures 2002* (Cambridge, UK: Cambridge University Press, 2002), 72–73.

26 See Gregory Mitchell and Philip E. Tetlock, "Antidiscrimination Law and the Perils of Mindreading," 67 *Ohio State Law Journal* 1023 (2006) and Melissa Hart, "Subjective Decision-making and Unconscious Discrimination," 56 *Alabama Law Review* 741 (2005).

27 Orlando Patterson, *The Ordeal of Integration: Progress and Resentment in America's "Racial" Crisis* (New York: Basic Civitas, 1997), 2.

28 Barry Schwartz and Kenneth Sharpe, *Practical Wisdom: The Right Way to Do the Right Thing* (New York: Riverhead, 2010), 6.

29 Jackson, Boostrom, and Hansen, *The Moral Life of Schools*, 34.

30 See Linda L. Putnam, "Productive Conflict: Negotiation as Implicit Coordination," in *Using Conflict in Organizations* (London: Sage Publications, 1997), 147: "Conflict in organizations promotes flexibility and adaptiveness, and prevents stagnation."

31 People never "attain the equality they desire," Tocqueville observed: "They constantly believe they are going to seize it, and it constantly escapes their grasp." Tocqueville, *Democracy in America*, 2:138–39.

32 Patterson, *The Ordeal of Integration*, 115.

33 See, e.g., Daniela Scur, et al. "The World Management Survey at 18: Lessons and the Way Forward," 37 *Oxford Review of Economic Policy* 2 (Summer 2021).

34 Peter F. Drucker, *Post-Capitalist Society* (New York: HarperCollins, 1994), 56.

35 See discussion in Howard, *The Rule of Nobody*, 96–110.

36 See discussion in the second ("The Human Authority Needed for Good Schools") and third ("Escape from Quicksand") essays of this book.

37 Oliver Wendell Holmes, Jr., *The Common Law* (Clark, NJ: Lawbook Exchange, 2005), 41.

[b] **Warnings for everything**: See discussion in Howard, *The Collapse of the Common Good*, 3–70.

"defensive medicine": See, e.g., Chad Terhune, "The $200 Billion Perils of Unnecessary Medical Tests," *PBS NewsHour*, May 24, 2017. See also Philip K. Howard, "Just Medicine," *New York Times*, April 1, 2009.

Job references: See discussion in Howard, *The Collapse of the Common Good*, 3–70.

"similar cases should be decided alike": Eugene V. Rostow, "American Legal Realism and the Sense of the Profession," 34 *Rocky Mountain Law Review* 123, 126 (1962).

"whim of the particular jury": Oliver Wendell Holmes, Jr., "Law in Science and Science in Law," 12 *Harvard Law Review* 443, 458 (1899).

"if it is *vulnerable* to legal action": Donald J. Black, "The Mobilization of Law," 2 *The Journal of Legal Studies* 125, 131 n. 24 (1973).

"Negligence . . . [is] a standard of conduct": Holmes, "Law in Science and Science in Law."

Conventional wisdom is that anyone has the right to bring a lawsuit and have the jury decide—that bringing lawsuits is an unfettered right, like freedom of speech. But lawsuits are an act of state power—just like indicting someone for a crime, except the claim is for money. We would never let a prosecutor seek the death penalty for a misdemeanor, so why do we allow, as in one crazy case, someone sue their dry cleaners for $54 million for a lost pair of pants? (See discussion in Howard, *Life Without Lawyers*, 72–73.) I have argued that judges not only have the inherent power, but the obligation, to make rulings on the boundaries of lawsuits. Legislatures could also require rulings. Here is language of a short statute that would explicitly require judges to make rulings when claims might affect the freedoms of people throughout society:

> Judges shall take the responsibility to draw the boundaries of reasonable dispute as a matter of law, applying common law principles and statutory guidelines. In making these rulings, judges shall consider the potential effects of claims on society at large.

38 **"authentically incompetent"**: Dunkelman, *Why Nothing Works*, 161.

Dreary public culture: See discussion in Howard, *Everyday Freedom*, 2 (and related notes); Howard, *Not Accountable*; and Philip K. Howard, "From Progressivism to Paralysis," 130 *The Yale Law Journal Forum* 370 (January 2021).

39 **150 million words**: See Philip K. Howard, "A Radical Centrist Platform for 2020," *The Hill*, April 13, 2019. The figure was calculated by multiplying the number of pages in the U.S. Code with the number of words in an average

page, then adding that figure to a similar calculation of the Code of Federal Regulations.

Joy dishwashing liquid: Philip K. Howard, *The Death of Common Sense: How Law Is Suffocating America* (New York: Random House, 1995), 36–38.

Study of historic buildings: See discussion of the rebuilding of the Bayonne Bridge in Howard, *The Rule of Nobody*, 7–12.

40 **Doctors and nurses:** See, e.g., Danielle Ofri, "The Patients vs. Paperwork Problem for Doctors," *New York Times*, November 14, 2017.

Special ed teachers: See, e.g., "Where Does Special Education Teachers (SET) Time Go?" *Frontline Education* (2018).

Homelessness: See, e.g., Eraklis A. Diamataris, "NYC's Homelessness Dilemma Rooted in Bureaucracy and Anti-Business Politics," *The National Herald*, November 23, 2023 (arguing that bureaucratic hurdles to building housing artificially constrain housing supply in New York City, exacerbating homelessness).

41 See, e.g., Weinstein, "How to Cut Administrative Bloat at U.S. Colleges" and Paul C. Light, *Thickening Government: Federal Hierarchy and the Diffusion of Accountability* (Washington, DC: Brookings Institution Press, 1995). University of Pittsburgh professor Jennifer Brick Murtazashvili discussed the bureaucratization of higher education at "The Day After DOGE," a forum

co-hosted by Columbia University's Richman Center and Common Good, April 23, 2025.

42 **"Abundance"**: See, e.g., Klein and Thompson, *Abundance.*

Privacy laws: Linda Miller of Program Integrity Alliance discussed how privacy laws hinder the catching of fraud and waste at "The Day After DOGE," a forum co-hosted by Columbia University's Richman Center and Common Good, April 23, 2025.

Multiple mandates: See discussion in the third essay of this book, "Escape from Quicksand," and Dunkelman, *Why Nothing Works.*

43 James Madison, speech in Congress on the Removal Power, May 19, 1789, in *Writings* (New York: Library of America: 1999), 435.

44 See discussion in Howard, *The Rule of Nobody*, 147–51 and in the third essay of this book, "Escape from Quicksand."

45 See discussion in the third essay of this book, "Escape from Quicksand."

46 **"social capital"**: See Robert D. Putnam, *Bowling Alone: The Collapse and Revival of American Community* (New York: Simon & Schuster, 2001), 18–19.

"obedience to . . . unenforceable": John Fletcher Moulton, "Law and Manners," *The Atlantic*, July 1942.

47 "**lost the distinction**": Alan Wolfe, *One Nation, After All: What Middle-Class Americans Really Think about God, Country, Family, Racism, Welfare, Immigration, Homosexuality, Work, the Right, the Left, and Each Other* (New York: Viking, 1998), 300.

"**But a society**": Aleksandr Solzhenitsyn, *Solzhenitsyn at Harvard: The Address, Twelve Early Responses, and Six Later Reflections*, ed. Ronald Berman (Washington, DC: Ethics and Public Policy Center, 1980), 8.

48 Václav Havel, *The Art of the Impossible* (New York: Knopf, 1997), 178.

49 "**The force of character**": Ralph Waldo Emerson, "Self-Reliance," in *Essays and Lectures* (New York: Library of America, 1983), 266.

"**My lived experience**": Wojtyla, "Subjectivity and the Irreducibile in the Human Being."

50 Robert Reich, *The Common Good* (New York: Knopf, 2018), 131–55.

51 Economist Garett Jones, in *The Culture Transplant* (Stanford, CA: Stanford Business Books, 2022) found that immigrants from different cultural traditions tend to stick to themselves and do not assimilate into the new society.

52 See Robert D. Putnam, "*E Pluribus Unum*: Diversity and Community in the Twenty-first Century," 30 *Scandinavian Political Studies* 137 (June 2007).

53 Havel, *The Art of the Impossible*, 91. The legalistic state disregards what Pope John Paul II called the "authentic personal subjectivity of the human being." Wojtyla, "Subjectivity and the Irreducible in the Human Being."

54 Havel, *The Art of the Impossible*, 92, 126.

55 Hayek, *The Constitution of Liberty*, 86.

56 "Freedom does not last long when bestowed from above," historian Arthur M. Schlesinger, Jr., observed in another context: "It lasts only when it is arrived at competitively." Arthur M. Schlesinger, Jr., *The Age of Jackson* (Boston: Little, Brown, 1953), 523.

57 Tocqueville, *Democracy in America*, 2:8. See also Prov. 29:18.

58 **Protecting individual freedom**: Locke, *The Second Treatise on Civil Government*, 33.

Regulations should be knowable: "It will be of little avail to the people," James Madison noted, "that the laws are made by men of their own choice, if the laws be so voluminous that they cannot be read, or so incoherent that they cannot be understood." James Madison, "Federalist No. 62," in Alexander Hamilton, John Jay, and James Madison, *The Federalist Papers* (Project Gutenberg eBook, 1998).

Regulations should leave room for officials: See discussion in the second ("The Human Authority Needed for Good Schools") and third ("Escape from Quicksand") essays of this book.

Law should not intercede in personal relations: See discussion in Howard, *The Collapse of the Common Good*, 173–98.

Law must be predictable: See Holmes, *The Common Law*, 41. Keeping law aligned with social norms of justice, as Benjamin Cardozo observed, "is a concept by far more subtle and indefinite than is yielded by mere obedience to a rule." Benjamin N. Cardozo, *The Growth of the Law* (New Haven, CT: Yale University Press, 1924), 87.

The Human Authority Needed for Good Schools

1   I have written about the importance of authority in institutions and in a free society, most recently in *Everyday Freedom: Designing the Framework for a Flourishing Society* (Garden City, NY: Rodin, 2024). See also Philip K. Howard, *Try Common Sense: Replacing the Failed Ideologies of Right and Left* (New York: W.W. Norton, 2019) and Philip K. Howard, *The Rule of Nobody: Saving America from Dead Laws and Broken Government* (New York: W.W. Norton, 2014).

2   See, e.g., Craig D. Jerald, "School Culture: 'The Hidden Curriculum,'" The Center for Comprehensive School Reform and Improvement (December 2006), https://files.eric.ed.gov/fulltext/ED495013.pdf; and discussion with former Rhode Island education commissioner Ken Wagner in Howard, *Everyday Freedom*, 17.

3   See, e.g., Ashley Rogers Berner, *Pluralism and American Public Education: No One Way to School* (New York: Palgrave Macmillan, 2017), 90–91.

4   Philip W. Jackson, Robert E. Boostrom, and David T. Hansen, *The Moral Life of Schools* (San Francisco: Jossey-Bass, 1998), 115.

5   Author's conversation with Jackie Pons, 2005; see also discussion in Philip K. Howard, *Life Without Lawyers: Restoring Responsibility in America* (New York: W.W. Norton, 2010), 115.

6   Frederick M. Hess, *The Great School Rethink* (Cambridge, MA: Harvard Education Press, 2023), 112.

7   Author's conversation with Eva Moskowitz, June 2024.

8   Sara Lawrence-Lightfoot, *The Good High School: Portraits of Character and Culture* (New York: Basic Books, 1983), 68.

9   Thomas Kelly, "Deborah Kenny: Radical Education Reformer," *Esquire* (November 19, 2007), *https://www.esquire.com/news-politics/a3955/kenny1207/*.

10   "The 2010 O Power List; Deborah Kenny: The Power of Smart," *O (The Oprah Magazine)*, September 14, 2010, https://web.archive.org/web/20100919151659/http://www.oprah.com/world/The-2010-O-Power-List/22.

11   Carl Campanile, "Charter Gets Perfect Score," *New York Post*, June 25, 2010, https://nypost.com/2010/06/25/charter-gets-perfect-score/.

12   Hess, *The Great School Rethink*, 112.

13 On spending, see "Education Expenditures by Country," National Center for Education Statistics (August 2023), https://nces.ed.gov/programs/coe/indicator/cmd/education-expenditures-by-country; on U.S. rankings, see "PISA 2022 Results (Volume I and II)–Country Notes: United States," Organisation for Economic Co-operation and Development (OECD), December 5, 2023, https://www.oecd.org/en/publications/pisa-2022-results-volume-i-and-ii-country-notes_ed6fbcc5-en/united-states_a78ba65a-en.html#chapter-d1e11.

14 Ted Dabrowski and John Klingner, "Education Fail: Not a Single Child Tested Proficient in Math in 67 Illinois Schools. For Reading, It's 32 Schools," Wirepoints, February 13, 2024, https://wirepoints.org/education-fail-not-a-single-child-tested-proficient-in-math-in-67-illinois-schools-for-reading-its-32-schools-wirepoints-special-report/.

15 David Osborne, *Reinventing America's Schools: Creating a 21st Century Education System* (New York: Bloomsbury, 2017), Kindle ed. Loc. 25.

16 See, e.g., "Factsheet: Education and Socioeconomic Status," American Psychological Association, https://www.apa.org/pi/ses/resources/publications/factsheet-education.pdf (summarizing research that finds, among other things, that socioeconomic status [SES] is a major determinant of educational achievement, but that low-SES students who are moved from low- to high-performing schools are able to significantly close the gap with their higher-SES peers).

17   See "NAEP Long-Term Trend Assessment Results: Reading and Mathematics," The Nation's Report Card, https://www.nationsreportcard.gov/ltt.

18   See discussion in Howard, *Everyday Freedom*, 1–6.

19   Alyssa Hadley Dunn, Matthew Deroo, and Jennifer VanDerHeide, "With Regret: The Genre of Teachers' Public Resignation Letters," *Linguistics and Education* 38 (2017): 37.

20   See Berner, *Pluralism and American Public Education*, 41; see also Jal Mehta, *The Allure of Order: High Hopes, Dashed Expectations, and the Troubled Quest to Remake American Schooling* (New York: Oxford University Press, 2013) (on how Taylorism infected Progressive Era ideas of schooling); and Osborne, *Reinventing America's Schools*, Kindle ed. Loc. 68.

21   See discussion in Philip K. Howard, *Not Accountable: Rethinking the Constitutionality of Public Employee Unions* (Garden City, NY: Rodin, 2023), 115–24.

22   See discussion in Philip K. Howard, *The Death of Common Sense: How Law Is Suffocating America* (New York: Random House, 2011), 161–63; see also Richard Arum, *Judging School Discipline: The Crisis of Moral Authority* (Cambridge, MA: Harvard University Press, 2003).

23   See discussion in Howard, *The Death of Common Sense*, 148–54.

24 See, e.g., Jamie Vollmer, "The Ever Increasing Burden of America's Public Schools," adapted for the Center on Regional Politics at Temple University (Summer 2014), https://sites.temple.edu/corparchives/files/2019/08/Vollmer-Bulletin-insert.pdf.

25 Daniel Buck, "California Will Teach Kids Anything Except How to Read," *Wall Street Journal*, June 21, 2024, https://www.wsj.com/articles/california-will-teach-kids-anything-except-how-to-read-education-babf9e9e.

26 Winnie Hu, "New York School Districts Challenge State Mandates," *New York Times*, April 14, 2011, https://www.nytimes.com/2011/04/15/nyregion/new-york-school-districts-challenge-state-mandates.html.

27 Dana Goldstein, "In Florida, New School Laws Have an Unintended Consequence: Bureaucracy," *New York Times*, January 10, 2024, https://www.nytimes.com/2024/01/10/us/florida-education-schools-laws.html.

28 Ken Futernick, "A Possible Dream: Retaining California Teachers So All Students Learn," California State University (2007): 17, https://web.archive.org/web/20070804064254/http:/www.calstate.edu/teacherquality/documents/possible_dream.pdf.

29 Hess, *The Great School Rethink*, 28.

30 Author's conversation with Ken Wagner, July 2023; see also discussion in Howard, *Everyday Freedom*, 1, 17.

31 Osborne, *Reinventing America's Schools*, Kindle ed. Loc. 34.

32 The corrosion of school culture by post-1960s controls is vividly described by Gerald Grant in *The World We Created at Hamilton High* (Cambridge, MA: Harvard University Press, 1990).

33 See discussion in Howard, *Not Accountable*, 59–70.

34 See Terry M. Moe, *Special Interest: Teachers Unions and America's Public Schools* (Washington, DC: Brookings Institution Press, 2011); Daniel DiSalvo, *Government against Itself: Public Union Power and Its Consequences* (New York: Oxford University Press, 2015); and Michael T. Hartney, *How Policies Make Interest Groups: Governments, Unions, and American Education* (Chicago: University of Chicago Press, 2022).

35 See Moe, *Special Interest*, 183.

36 "Providence Public School District: A Review," Johns Hopkins Institute for Education Policy (June 2019): 62–63, https://jscholarship.library.jhu.edu/server/api/core/bitstreams/598f7a85-c7ea-4155-9983-5e565ddc2698/content.

37 See discussion in Philip K. Howard, *The Collapse of the Common Good: How America's Lawsuit Culture Undermines Our Freedom* (New York: Ballantine, 2001), 123.

38 Frederick Hess, "Teacher Quality, Teacher Pay," Hoover Institution (April 1, 2004), https://www.hoover.org/research/teacher-quality-teacher-pay.

39 See, e.g., John Martin, "District's 'Teacher of the Year' laid off," CNN.com, June 14, 2012, https://www.cnn.com/2012/06/14/us/districts-teacher-of-the-year-laid-off; and Jill Barshay, "As Teacher Layoffs Loom, Research Evidence Mounts That Seniority Protections Hurt Kids in Poverty," The Hechinger Report, June 10, 2024, https://hechingerreport.org/proof-points-teacher-layoffs-seniority-protections/.

40 Steven Brill, Tailspin: *The People and Forces behind America's Fifty-Year Fall—and Those Fighting to Reverse It* (New York: Knopf, 2018), 265–66. See also discussion in Howard, *Try Common Sense*, 93–95.

41 Moe, *Special Interest*, 186.

42 Author's conversation with Ryan Hill, 2008; see discussion in Howard, *Life Without Lawyers*, 122.

43 See, e.g., Jeffrey Liker and Michael Hoseus, *Toyota Culture: The Heart and Soul of the Toyota Way* (New York: McGraw-Hill, 2008), 414–18.

44 Howard, *Not Accountable*, 30–36; see also Philip K. Howard, "Why Government Unions—Unlike Trade Unions—Corrupt Democracy," *Time*, April 4, 2023, https://time.com/6267979/government-unions-corrupt-democracy/.

45 DiSalvo, *Government against Itself*, 60 (citing Moe, *Special Interest*, 292–93).

46   See discussion in Howard, *Not Accountable*, 127–46.

47   See, e.g., Greg Forster and Christian D'Andrea, "Free to Teach: What America's Teachers Say about Teaching in Public and Private Schools," The Friedman Foundation for Educational Choice, May 2009, https://files.eric.ed.gov/fulltext/ED508314.pdf; Christopher Small and David G. Buckman, "Public and Private Schools: A Study of Teacher Job Satisfaction," *ICPEL Education Leadership Review* 22, no. 1 (December 2021); and Soheyla Taie and Laurie Lewis, "Characteristics of 2020–21 Public and Private K–12 School Teachers in the United States: Results from the National Teacher and Principal Survey," U.S. Department of Education, NCES 2022-113 (December 2022): A-12-14, https://nces.ed.gov/pubs2022/2022113.pdf.

48   See discussion in Howard, *Not Accountable*, 17–23.

49   Peter F. Drucker, *The Essential Drucker: The Best of Sixty Years of Peter Drucker's Essential Writings on Management* (New York: Harper Business, 2003), 221.

50   As I have argued in a number of books, these governing frameworks are also in need of overhaul.

51   Katherine Schaeffer, "U.S. Public, Private and Charter Schools in 5 Charts," Pew Research Center, June 6, 2024, https://www.pewresearch.org/short-reads/2024/06/06/us-public-private-and-charter-schools-in-5-charts/.

52   See Frederick Winslow Taylor, *The Principles of Scientific Management* (New York: W.W. Norton, 1967).

53 Gary Hamel and Michele Zanini, "Harnessing Everyday Genius," *Harvard Business Review* (July–August 2020), https://hbr.org/2020/07/harnessing-everyday-genius; and author's conversation with Michele Zanini, July 2024.

54 Hamel and Zanini, "Harnessing Everyday Genius."

55 See Liker and Hoseus, *Toyota Culture*; Hamel and Zanini, "Harnessing Everyday Genius"; and Gary Hamel and Michele Zanini, "The End of Bureaucracy," *Harvard Business Review* (November–December 2018), https://hbr.org/2018/11/the-end-of-bureaucracy.

56 See John Braithwaite and Valerie Braithwaite, "The Politics of Legalism: Rules versus Standards in Nursing-Home Regulation," *Social & Legal Studies* 4, no. 3 (1995): 307–41. For additional discussion, see generally Howard, *The Rule of Nobody*.

57 Author's conversation with Paul Hill, July 2024.

58 See "Phased Out: As the City Closed Low-Performing Schools How Did Their Students Fare?," New York City Independent Budget Office (January 2016), https://www.ibo.nyc.ny.us/iboreports/phased-out-as-the-city-closed-low-performing-schools-how-did-their-students-fare-jan-2016.pdf; see also Howard S. Bloom, Saskia Levy Thompson, and Rebecca Unterman, "Transforming the High School Experience: How New York City's New Small Schools Are Boosting Student Achievement and Graduation Rates," MDRC, June 2010, https://www.mdrc.org/sites/default/files/full_589.pdf.

59 Studies of efforts at cultural reform in business find that just over 10 percent meet their goals. That's mainly because, management expert Michele Zanini told me, the reforms are usually instituted from the top down instead of empowering employees down the line and terminating those who don't adapt to the new responsibility.

60 See Thomas Ahn and Jacob Vigdor, "The Impact of No Child Left Behind's Accountability Sanctions on School Performance: Regression Discontinuity Evidence from North Carolina," National Bureau of Economic Research, Working Paper 20511, September 2014, www.nber.org/papers/w20511.

61 Charles M. Payne, *So Much Reform, So Little Change: The Persistence of Failure in Urban Schools* (Cambridge, MA: Harvard Education Press, 2008), 197.

62 Berner, *Pluralism and American Public Education*, 91.

63 Douglas N. Harris and Matthew F. Larsen, "Taken by Storm: The Effects of Hurricane Katrina on Medium-Term Student Outcomes in New Orleans," Education Research Alliance for New Orleans (July 15, 2018, updated May 17, 2021): 3–6, 22, 52, https://educationresearchalliancenola.org/files/publications/Harris-Larsen-Reform-Effects-2021-05-17.pdf.

64 Osborne, *Reinventing America's Schools*, Kindle ed. Loc. 65.

65 Osborne, *Reinventing America's Schools*, Kindle ed. Loc. 51.

Escape from Quicksand: A New Framework for Modernizing America

1 See Shannon Osaka, "Biden's $7.5 Billion Investment in EV Charging Has Only Produced 7 Stations in Two Years," *Washington Post*, March 28, 2024; Grant Schwab, Kalea Hall, and Luke Ramseth, "$5B for EV Infrastructure Yields Just 11 Charging Stations," *Governing*, July 2, 2024. [AU: months spelled out for consistency with previous endnotes styling]

2 "The Harris Broadband Rollout Has Been a Fiasco," editorial, *Wall Street Journal*, October 4, 2024.

3 Michael Grunwald, *The New New Deal: The Hidden Story of Change in the Obama Era* (New York: Simon & Schuster, 2012), 305–10.

4 Michael B. Gerrard, "A Time for Triage," *Environmental Forum* 39, no. 6 (November–December 2022): 38–44. See also Johanna Bozuwa et al., "Planning to Build Faster: A Solar Energy Case Study," Roosevelt Institute, October 1, 2024. This report, which explicitly disavows the need to make trade-offs, demonstrates the disconnection from reality of some environmentalists: "Our approach to looking for land-sparing opportunities draws from research on techno-ecological synergies, offering opportunities to multi-solve across ecological and technological domains to *avoid trade-offs* and instead embrace multifunctional landscapes" (emphasis added).

In a review of the report, Matthew Yglesias, "Tradeoffs Are Real," *Slow Boring* (blog), October 15, 2024, writes that he "felt like I'd gone insane" because "every recommendation the report makes would make solar slower and more expensive to make."

5 Michael D. Shear, "Obama Lesson: 'Shovel Ready' Not So Ready," *New York Times*, October 15, 2010. See also Jonathan Alter, *The Promise: President Obama, Year One* (New York: Simon & Schuster, 2010), 89, which notes that then-president-elect Obama was "appalled" to learn that his proposal for a national smart grid would require the approval of at least 231 state and local agencies. "We went to the moon!" he said.

6 Philip K. Howard, "Two Years, Not Ten Years: Redesigning Infrastructure Approvals," Common Good, September 15, 2015.

7 Fixing America's Surface Transportation (FAST) Act, Pub. L. No. 114–94, 129 Stat. 1312 (2015).

8 Senator Joe Manchin, "Manchin, Portman, Sinema, Sullivan Introduce Bill to Improve Federal Permitting Process, Create Jobs" (July 13, 2021).

9 Philip Rossetti, "Addressing NEPA-Related Infrastructure Delays," R Street Policy Institute, July 2021.

10 Among many other things, the Infrastructure Investment and Jobs Act of 2021 (IIJA) imposed two-year time limits on environmental reviews for transportation

infrastructure projects, as well as page limits for the environmental impact statement (EIS) for those projects. However, both these requirements are relatively easy to waive. IIJA also reiterated the FAST Act's judicial review reforms (two-year statute of limitations and requirement that lawsuits be filed only by parties who had submitted a comment during the environmental review). Infrastructure Investment and Jobs Act, Pub. L. No. 117-58, § 80503, 135 Stat. 429, 1336 (2021) (to be codified at 26 U.S.C. § 7451).

Two years later, the Fiscal Responsibility Act of 2023 (FRA) directly modified the National Environmental Policy Act (NEPA) by imposing time and page limits on all federal environmental reviews, not just those in the transportation sector, although here too the requirements are easy to waive. FRA also allows agencies to share categorical exclusions they have developed and allows project sponsors to sue to compel agencies to stick to established permitting timelines. FRA, Pub. L. No. 118–5, 173 Stat. 10 (2023).

As of the time of this essay's publication, two noteworthy permitting reform bills are working their way through Congress. In the Senate, the Energy Permitting Reform Act of 2024, sponsored by Senators Manchin and Barrasso, would expand the use of categorical exclusions for a variety of energy projects, empower the Federal Energy Regulatory Commission to issue permits for regionally significant transmission projects (preempting state authority), impose deadlines on several permitting processes, and tighten statutes of limitations for challenges to agency actions. Energy Permitting Reform Act, S.4753, 118th Cong. (2024).

In the House, an as-yet-unnamed bill introduced by Congressman Westerman would limit environmental reviews to issues within the lead agency's jurisdiction, exempt grants and loans from the NEPA process, and limit injunctive relief only to those situations where there is a risk of "proximate and substantial environmental harm" from allowing the project to proceed. A discussion draft of this untitled, unnumbered bill: https://docs.house.gov/meetings/II/II00/20240911/117585/BILLS-118pih-ToamendtheNationalEnvironmentalPolicyActof1969andforotherpurposes.pdf.

11 Harold Meyerson, "Work History," *American Prospect*, May 2, 2010.

12 James M. Landis, *The Administrative Process* (New Haven, CT: Yale University Press, 1938), 75. See discussion in Howard, "From Progressivism to Paralysis."

13 James Madison, speech in Congress on the Removal Power, May 19, 1789, in *Writings* (New York: Library of America, 1999), 435.

14 National Environmental Policy Act (NEPA), 42 U.S.C. §§ 4321–47 (1970).

15 See, e.g., Daniel A. Dreyfus, "NEPA: The Original Intent of the Law," *Journal of Professional Issues in Engineering Education and Practice* 109, no. 4 (1983): 252–53.

16 *Kleppe v. Sierra Club*, 427 U.S. 390 at 410 (1976).

17   See Marc J. Dunkelman, *Why Nothing Works* (New York: Public Affairs, 2025), 266–68. California's environmental review law requires that "cities *mitigate* whatever environmental impacts might occur from local land use decisions" (227), including "to address nearly one hundred issues—noise, endangered species, traffic. . . . And opponents simply need to find a flaw in one to put the entire project on ice. A plan to turn an old, polluted aircraft manufacturing facility in Los Angeles onto a vibrant new development with housing, office space, and a park was subject to twenty CEQA suits over twenty years" (231).

18   Dunkelman, *Why Nothing Works*, provides numerous examples of how "project opponents invok[e] environmental concerns as the thinnest veneer for naked self-interest."

19   Council on Environmental Quality, "Environmental Impact Statement Timelines, 2010–2018," June 12, 2020.

20   See Nikki Chiappa et al., "Understanding NEPA Litigation," Breakthrough Institute, July 11, 2024, which finds that, on average, 4.2 years elapsed between the filing of a final EIS and conclusion of related litigation.

21   Adam Van Brimmer and Zachariah Chou, "Timeline: The Savannah Harbor Expansion Project Was a Deep—and Lengthy—Dig," *Savannah Morning News*, February 25, 2022. Dunkelman, *Why Nothing Works*, provides detailed biopsy of decade-long efforts to block a transmission line running from Canada across Maine—including thirty-eight permits, multiple lawsuits, and voter referenda (279–91).

22   See Shawn Regan, "The L.A. Wildfires Should Be a Wake-up Call," *City Journal*, January 10, 2025; Scott Dittrich, letter to the editor, "A Malibu Official on the California Wildfires," *Wall Street Journal*, January 21, 2025. Cape Wind, which would have been the country's first offshore wind farm, survived more than two dozen lawsuits over sixteen years, but was scrapped in 2017 after the delay made it economically unviable. See Katharine Q. Seelye, "After 16 Years, Hopes for Cape Cod Wind Farm Float Away," *New York Times*, December 19, 2017; Cynthia E. Stead, "The Hypocrisy of Cape Wind Opponents," *Cape Cod Times*, January 13, 2015.

23   See *City of Port Isabel v. Federal Energy Regulatory Comm.*, 111 F.4th 1198, 1206–1211 (2024). See also Greg LaRose, "Appeals Court Sends Louisiana LNG Terminal Project Back to Regulators," *Louisiana Illuminator*, July 16, 2024; *Healthy Gulf v. FERC*, 107 F.4th 1033 (U.S. Ct. of Appeals, D.C. Cir., July 16, 2024).

24   Cathy Landry, "Court Orders Federal Agency to Better Protect Rice's Whales from Oil, Gas Drilling in Gulf of Mexico," *Oil & Gas Journal*, August 21, 2024; *Sierra Club v. Nat'l Marine Fisheries Service*, Civ. No. DLB-20-3060 (U.S. Dist. Ct., D. Md., Jan. 9, 2024).

25   See Howard, *Everyday Freedom*, 20.

26   The conceit of procedural decision-making is that a correct solution will emerge from all the study and discussion. But it's impossible to demonstrate, as a matter of

objective evidence, the wisdom of necessary choices. The powers of reasoning, as neuroscientist Antonio Damasio explains, will spin endlessly unless people can access a different part of the brain, where people draw on their emotions and decide how to act. Antonio Damasio, *Descartes' Error: Emotion, Reason and the Human Brain* (New York: Penguin, 1994). Information can inform these judgments, but usually only to a modest degree. Timing also requires a value judgment about trade-offs—whether the costs of further process outweigh the potential benefits. Some official must have authority to make these judgments.

27 People generally make poorer decisions, organizational psychologists have found, when they know they must give reasons to justify their judgments. Throw in the near-certainty of a legal challenge, and the illusory standard of objective proof, and the result is inexorable pressure toward the lowest common denominator. The process skews decisions toward mollifying the squeaky wheels. After a while, officials lose any clear line of sight toward the greater good. After seventeen years, BNSF railroad finally gave up on building a large intermodal transfer facility near the port of Long Beach, which would have dramatically reduced truck congestion and pollution, because of an inability to overcome local objections.

28 Ezra Klein, "A Close Examination of the Most Infamous Public Toilet in America," *New York Times*, April 28, 2024.

29 Jennifer Pahlka, "Democrats Should Be the Party of Go," *Eating Policy* (Substack blog), August 26, 2024.

30 Ibid.

31 Jennifer Pahlka, "AI Meets the Cascade of Rigidity," in *The Digitalist Papers*, ed. Angela Aristidou (Stanford, CA: Stanford Digital Economy Lab, 2024).

32 Steven Kelman, *Procurement and Public Management: The Fear of Discretion and the Quality of Government Performance* (Washington, DC: AEI Press, 1990), 52.

33 Václav Havel, "The End of the Modern Era," *New York Times*, March 1, 1992.

34 See Howard, *Everyday Freedom*.

35 Chester I. Barnard, *The Functions of the Executive: Thirtieth Anniversary Edition* (Cambridge, MA: Harvard University Press, 1968), 232.

36 See discussion on procurement procedures in Howard, *The Death of Common Sense*, 62–76.

37 Author interviews with housing developers from Los Angeles and Dallas.

38 Kelman, *Procurement and Public Management*, 52.

39 Brendan Carr, "Kamala Harris's Rural Broadband Flop," *Wall Street Journal*, October 14, 2024.

40 Brian M. Rosenthal, "The Most Expensive Mile of Subway Track on Earth," *New York Times*, December 28, 2017.

41 See discussion and sources in Howard, *The Rule of Nobody*, 116.

42 See Howard, *Everyday Freedom*, 59–63.

43 See, e.g., Brad L. Utter, *Enterprising Waters: The History and Art of New York's Erie Canal* (Albany: State University of New York Press, 2020).

44 See, e.g., *After Promontory: One Hundred and Fifty Years of Transcontinental Railroading*, ed. Keith L. Bryant, Jr. (Bloomington: Indiana University Press, 2020).

45 Federal Aid Highway Act of 1956, Pub. L. No. 84-627 (1956).

46 See Jim Hook, "I-81 History: States Scramble to Be the First as Construction Begins," *The Sentinel*, January 15, 2011.

47 Former EPA general counsel E. Donald Elliott has counted more than fifty statutes that grant "categorical exclusions" in critical situations, plus "hundreds" more created by agencies for a wide variety of actions—e.g., asbestos abatement, refueling nuclear reactors, or decommissioning naval vessels. See "Hearing on Permitting Litigation Efficiency Act of 2018 Before H. Comm. on the Judiciary, Subcomm. on Regulatory Reform, Commercial and Antitrust" (statement of E. Donald Elliott), 115th Cong. (April 12, 2018); see also Council on Environmental Quality, "List of Federal Agency Categorical Exclusions."

48 See Energy Permitting Reform Act.

49 See Meyerson, "Work History"; Charles Peters and Timothy Noah, "Wrong Harry: Four Million Jobs in Two Years? FDR Did It in Two Months," *Slate*, January 26, 2009.

50 See Jennifer Pahlka and Andrew Greenway, "The How We Need Now: A Capacity Agenda for 2025 and Beyond," Niskanen Center, December 2024, a report proposing a four-step approach to expediting decisions: "hire the right people and fire the wrong ones"; "reduce procedural bloat"; "invest in digital infrastructure"; and "close the feedback loop between policy and implementation." But it offers no theory of authority to resolve disagreements, no authority to waive or modify the countless regulations that might prevent trade-off judgments, and no principle to limit judicial review and delay.

51 Former EPA general counsel E. Donald Elliott has suggested removing the power of courts to issue preliminary injunctive relief, as provided in Section 307 of the Clean Air Act:

> **(g) Stay, injunction, or similar relief in proceedings relating to noncompliance penalties**
>
> In any action respecting the promulgation of regulations under section 7420 of this title or the administration or enforcement of section 7420 of this title no court shall grant any stay, injunctive, or similar relief before final judgment by such court in such action.

Litigation should also be expedited. In order to quickly resolve insinuations of bad faith, without years of legal discovery, all non-privileged files by litigants should be publicly disclosed at the outset of litigation. Complete transparency not only saves years of litigation but largely obviates the need for corrective environmental statements. All arguments will be in the open.

52 Businesses make investments in infrastructure and assets all the time, but the dynamics of accountability are completely different. Avoiding decisions is not an option, and accountability is unavoidable: What did the investment return to the bottom line? How do businesses figure out the right decision? They accept the unavoidable uncertainty, discuss differences of opinion, and make a decision. A leadership principle at Amazon is: "Have Backbone: Disagree and Commit." Sometimes it works out, sometimes it doesn't, and usually the projects must be altered in some way to meet unforeseen complications.

53 Diplomat George Kennan once proposed a fourth branch of government that would have no power but would report on how the other branches were doing. His "Council of State" comprised nine citizens "of high distinction" without political position or aspiration; its role was to provide a pillar of moral authority to reduce the incentives for political grandstanding. See George F. Kennan, *Around the Cragged Hill: A Personal and Political Philosophy* (New York: W.W. Norton, 1993), 238–48.

54 See "Infrastructure Australia: About Us," https://www.infrastructureaustralia.gov.au/about-us. Australia is not the only country with an infrastructure board. See, e.g.,

"Our Work," New Zealand Infrastructure Commission / Te Waihanga, https://tewaihanga.govt.nz/our-work; National Infrastructure Commission of the United Kingdom, "What We Do"; Infrastructure South Africa, "Our Vision and Mission."

55 The Uniform Commercial Code was drafted in the 1950s by a group of leading commercial law experts, led by Karl Llewellyn. Inspired by recodifications in Germany at the turn of the twentieth century, the code was adopted by almost every state and is a cornerstone of U.S. commercial law. See Lawrence M. Friedman, "Business Law in an Age of Change," in idem, *American Law in the 20th Century* (New Haven, CT: Yale University Press, 2022).

56 See, e.g., U.S. Dept. of Defense, "DoD Base Realignment and Closure," April 2022.

57 Aaron Gordon, "NJ Transit Train Fiasco Traps Commuters for Hours with No AC in Tunnel," *Bloomberg*, August 2, 2024.

58 See Philip K. Howard, "Billions for Red Tape: Focusing on the Approval Process for the Gateway Rail Project," Common Good (May 2016).

59 In 2017, environmental review was complete and needed only official approval from the secretary of transportation. But Trump reputedly didn't want to give a "win" to Democratic senators from New York and New Jersey, and the application languished until Biden was elected.

Trump's refusal to move the project forward should have been a scandal, but there was no oversight body, such as a national infrastructure board, to call him on it. See Tara Golshan, "Gateway, the Infrastructure Project Trump Hates So Much He Threatened a Shutdown, Explained," *Vox*, March 22, 2018.

60 Kevin R. Wexler, "Gateway Hudson Tunnel Project on Track for 2038 Completion," *Bergen Record*, May 21, 2024.

61 American Society of Civil Engineers (ASCE), 2025 Infrastructure Report Card.

62 ASCE, 2021 Infrastructure Report Card.

63 Jennifer Pahlka has documented how the bureaucratic culture is already busy weighing down decisions on artificial intelligence with "controls and mandates designed primarily to keep bad things from happening."

64 Aaron Bloom et al., "The Value of Increased HVDC Capacity Between Eastern and Western U.S. Grids: The Interconnection Seam Study," *IEEE Transactions on Power Systems* 37, no. 3 (May 2022): 1760–69.

65 ASCE, "Wastewater 2021."

ACKNOWLEDGMENTS

These essays, and particularly the introduction, profited from discussions with Philip Bobbitt and the feedback from participants at the Institute for Law & Strategy.

The "Striving" essay was improved by close reads and suggestions by Sean Brady, John Ketcham, Tony Kiser, Jonathan Leaf, Derek Leebaert, Ted Leonhardt, Jennifer Murtazashvili, and Conrad Scott. Daniela Scur provided a road map to studies on manageability. The essay was inspired by a forum co-sponsored by the Richman Center at Columbia University, organized by Daniela Tisch. I profited from the insights of Marc Dunkelman, Francis Fukuyama, Jeremy Kessler, Zach Liscow, Linda Miller, Chuck Sabel, David Schizer, Ilya Shapiro, and Michele Zanini.

"The Human Authority Needed for Good Schools" was commissioned by Hoover Institution, on the recommendation of Mitch Daniels, and profited from thoughtful comments by Macke Raymond, Stephen Bowen, and Hoover's excellent team. I thank also Jim Blew, Bob Eitel, Rick Hess, Paul Hill, David Osborne, Eva Moskowitz, Kathleen Porter-Magee, and David Steiner for the time they spent with me.

"Escape from Quicksand" was commissioned by the Milstein Innovation for Infrastructure Project at the Manhattan Institute, and profited from regular feedback from John Ketcham. Jennifer Pahlka generously read and reacted to several drafts. Don Elliott was always there to read and offer thoughtful suggestions.

I couldn't do this without the Common Good team—particularly the research by Andy Park, Matt Brown, and Seth Karecha, the thoughtful reactions of Henry Miller, and the team who organizes our activities, particularly Ruth Mary Giverin and Donna Thompson. Board members Tony Kiser, Scott Smith, and the late Greg Kennedy, advisory board member Larry Mone, and friends Dick Cashin and Fritz Hobbs helped raise the funds needed to make this work possible.

Arthur Klebanoff at Rodin Books had the idea for a book of essays. His excellent team, led by David Wilk at Booktrix and Michelle Weyenberg, made it come to fruition.

Thank you, always, to Alexandra.

ABOUT THE AUTHOR

Philip K. Howard is a lawyer, author, and chair of Common Good (www.commongood.org), a nonpartisan organization aimed at replacing red tape with human responsibility. He grew up in Kentucky and lives in New York City.